CONTENTS

INTRODUCTION

The eyes of the world were firmly fixed upon the new Duchess of Sussex, even before her idyllic wedding to Prince Harry in May 2018. But who is this enigmatic new Royal – and what drove her to become the formidable woman we see today?

Even when she was simply Meghan Markle, a successful American actress who just happened to be dating Britain's most eligible bachelor, there was always something special about Meghan that captured attention across the globe.

In fact, long before she started making UK newspaper headlines thanks to her Royal boyfriend, Meghan was turning heads as both a TV star and an active humanitarian.

From the moment this confident young lady stepped into the spotlight, it was clear that she was an inspiring role model: a self-made woman with beauty, grace, charm and an admirable devotion to philanthropic pursuits – qualities which marked her as a perfect candidate to become both a princess and a grounding life-partner for Harry, the Royal Family's lovable but most rebellious son.

But Meghan's life certainly hasn't always been a fairytale. The gritty girl from LA lived through the heartbreak of her parents' divorce when she was just six years old, while her adolescence was punctuated by a struggle to make sense of her biracial identity.

Meghan's mother Doria Ragland is a yoga instructor and therapist living in Los Angeles. Her father is Thomas W Markle Sr, a retired Emmy-award-winning lighting director and cameraman.

Growing up with a black mother and white father, Meghan has often reflected how, as a child, she never knew which box to tick on forms recording ethnicity. In those days the only choices available were white, black, Hispanic or Asian – there wasn't a specific box for mixed race. "So, I didn't tick a box. I left my identity blank – a question mark, an absolute incomplete –

much like how I felt," she explained in an article written for *Elle* magazine.

It was Meghan's father who first encouraged her to embrace her mixed-race status, telling her defiantly, "If that happens again, you draw your own box."

Indeed, Meghan's biracial upbringing and, in particular, the experience of seeing prejudice being directed toward her mother's side of the family have been integral in shaping her world view. Meghan reflected on racist incidents endured by her maternal grandfather and her own beloved mother Doria, on her now-defunct lifestyle website *The Tig*, "It reminds

MEGHAN

THE LIFE AND STYLE OF A
MODERN ROYAL

CAROLINE JONES

CARLTON
BOOKS

THIS IS A CARLTON BOOK

Published in 2019 by Carlton Books
An imprint of the Carlton Publishing Group
20 Mortimer Street
London W1T 3JW

Text © Caroline Jones 2019
Design © Carlton Books 2019

A CIP catalogue for this book is available from the British Library.

ISBN 978-1-78739-243-4

Printed in Dubai

10 9 8 7 6 5 4 3 2 1

Cover photographs: Alamy, Cartier, Self-Portrait, Getty Images, Jimmy Choo, REX/Shutterstock & Stathberry

Front Cover Top left: Galanterie de Cartier earrings, worn on her wedding day. Top middle: Self-Portrait dress worn to the Invictus Games. Top right: At the UN Women's Conference 2015. Middle: At her first post-wedding engagement with the Queen. Bottom left: The Your Commonwealth Youth Challenge reception. Bottom middle: Strathberry East/West Mini bag in bottle green, worn on her first official visit to Scotland. Bottom right: Jimmy Choo Romy 100 pumps, worn on a trip to Northern Ireland.

Back Cover Left: At the centenary celebrations for the RAF in London. Top right: At the launch of the Hubb Community kitchen cookbook, profits of which will help those affected by the Grenfell Tower fire. Bottom right: At an event aimed at inspiring the next generation of young women in STEM. Bottom left: Jimmy Choo J Box clutch bag, worn by Meghan to an Anzac Day service.

The publishers would like to thank the following sources for their kind permission to reproduce the pictures in this book.

Alamy: AF Archive 87 (centre); /Age Fotostock 148; /Uliana Bazar 140; /Oksana Bratanova 116 (right); /Matthew Chattle 161; /Forget-Gautier 121 (top); /ImageBroker 147 (top); /Image Source 145 (bottom); /Danny Martindale/WENN.com 70; /Patti McConville 123 (right); /RollingNews.ie 138; /Felix Shoughi 123 (left); /Agenzia Sintesi 118; /Wenn Ltd 13, 120 (top); /Liam White 22

Avalon/Photoshot: Pacific Coast News 82

Getty Images: 92 (left), 92 (bottom), 117 (right), 168; /Jonathan Brady/Pool 24 (top); /Frederick M. Brown 8 (top), 48; /Dan Charity/WPA Pool 73, 151; /Mike Coppola 130 (bottom); /Mark Cuthbert/UK Press 58; /Adrian Dennis/AFP 74 (left); /Amanda Edwards 50 (left); /Gareth Fuller/Pool 68 (left); /Sylvain Gaboury/Patrick McMullan 18; /Tim Graham 20 (top); /Samir Hussein/Wirelmage 5, 45 (right), 47, 77 (right), 147 (centre), 174; /Chris Jackson 1, 39 (left), 64, 71, 91, 167, 169, 171 (bottom); /Yale Joel/The LIFE Picture Collection 28; /Georges De Keerle 20 (bottom); /Robert W. Kelley/The LIFE Picture Collection 26; /Danny Lawson/AFP 17, /Daniel Leal-Olivas/AFP 44 (bottom left); /Dean Lewins/AFP 172; /Andrew Matthews/WPA Pool 54; /Kevin Mazur/Wirelmage 21; /Marty Melville 16; /Hannah McKay/WPA Pool 122; /Patrick McMullan 18; /Charles McQuillan 69 (top), 94; /Mark Mitchell 173; /Paul Morigi/Wirelmage 51 (top); /Indranil Mukherjee 158; /Max Mumby/Indigo 39, 42, 43, 52 (bottom), 69 (bottom), 72 (left), 162; /Cathy Murphy 29; /Win McNamee/ 19 (top); /Desiree Navarro/Wirelmage 95 (bottom left); /Phil Noble/Pool 171 (top); /Andrew Parsons/Pool 75 (right); /Steve Parsons/WPA Pool 55; /George Pimentel/Wirelmage 77 (left); /Todd Plitt 24; /David Rose/WPA Pool 165; /Jim Spellman/Wirelmage 51 (bottom); /Jeff Spicer 31; /Ben Stansall/WPA 8 (bottom); /John Thys/AFP 39 (right); /Michael Tullberg 52 (left); /Karwai Tang/Wirelmage 52 (right), 66, 88, 166; /Kirsty Wigglesworth/Pool 170

PA Images: 73 (right)

REX/Shutterstock: 4, 15, 30, 44 (left), 55 (bottom right), 56, 67, 68 (right), 75 (left), 80, 87 (top), 95 (top), 95 (bottom right); /AP 27; /Beretta/Sims 63; /Canadian Press 156; /Dominic Chan/Sipa USA 14 (top); /Alan Davidson 46, 74 (right); /ERPhotog 149 (top); /Billy Farrell Agency 50 (right); /Ronnybas Frimages 141; /Zach Gibson/AP 19 (bottom); /Jenny Goodall/Associated Newspapers 121 (bottom); /James Gourley/BPI 61; /Granger 23; /David Hartley 53 (centre right); /

Ken McKay/ITV 83; /Nieboer/PPE/SIPA 62; /Greg Pace 51; /Paramount/Kobal 90 (bottom); /Picture Perfect 49; /Geoff Robinson Photography 40; /Jack Robinson 25; /Tim Rooke 14 (bottom), 41, 53 (top left), 53 (bottom centre), 57, 60 (right), 65, 88, 90 (top), 159, 163; /Jeff Spicer 59; /Ben Stansall/AP 105; /Graham Stone 164; /Mark Parren Taylor 120 (bottom); /Carl Timpone/BFA 85; /USA Network/Netflix/Kobal 6; /Warner Bros/Kobal 60 (left)

Shutterstock: Africa Studio 115 (left), 153 (bottom); /Ana Iacob Photography 113; /Tono Balaguer 146; /Rudy Balasko 152 (top right); /CatchaSnap 106; /Karpenkov Denis 114; /J-Chizhe 115; /George Dolgikh 134 (left); /Domaine (top); /Tatyana Dzemileva 93 (centre); /Gemphoto 83; /Kristvin Gudmundsso 149 (bottom); /Arina P Habich 111; /Hannahmariah 131; /Irina02 127 (bottom); /Jasper. Z 144 (centre); /Jess Kraft 152 (bottom); /Lals Stock 152 (top left); /Boiarkina Marina 117 (centre); /Kostikova Natalia 130 (top); /Lisovskaya Natalia 117 (top); /Nattika 117; /OndroM 133; /Alena Ozerova 126; /Photographee.eu 128 (bottom); /Maksym Povozniuk 92 (top); /Suzi Pratt 107; /Alexander Prokopenko 110; /George Rudy 86 (bottom); /Sergio Monti Photography 150; /Shurkin Son 93 (top); /SpeedKingz 112 (bottom); /Jojo Textures 128 (top); /TheRunoman 144 (top); /Topseller 152 (bottom right); /Trabantos 145; /WorldWide 127 (Top), 132

Solo Syndication: 12

Unsplash: Alisa Anton 135; /Larisa Blinova 109; /Sarah Boyle 108; /Peter Bucks 134 (right); /Edgar Castrejon 86 (top); /Francesco Gallarotti 84; /Brent Hofacker 112; /Jared Rice 87 (bottom); /Crystal Shaw 129

World Vision: 7, 157

Special thank you to Paul Andrew, Bvlgari, Cartier, Caudalie, Chanel, CHIVA, Jimmy Choo, Decléor, Domaine Eden, Dr Bronner, Essie, Estee Lauder, Fresh, Cynthia Rowley, Dior, Judith & Charles, Kerastase, Mackage, Laura Mercier, Le Labo, Mac Comsmetics, Madewell, Make Up For Ever, Marlton, Mother, Nars Cosmetics, Natural Selection, Nivea, Pamuk & Co, Parosh, Revitalash, Rimmel, Sanctuary, Sentaler, Strathberry, Tatcha, Talika, Charlotte Tilbury, Vanessa Tugendhaft, Yves Saint Laurent, Wella, Wolford

Every effort has been made to acknowledge correctly and contact the source and/or copyright holder of each picture and Carlton Publishing Group apologises for any unintentional errors or omissions, which will be corrected in future editions of this book.

me of how young our country is. How far we've come and how far we still have to come."

This feeling of "otherness" and wanting to fit in appears to have filtered through into Meghan's early adulthood, a period during which she was often filled with self-doubt. In her own words: "My 20s were brutal – a constant battle with myself, judging my weight, my style, my desire to be as cool/as hip/as smart/as whatever as everyone else."

And yet it is these very struggles – and the strength of mind with which she eventually overcame them – that helped transform the young angst-filled Meghan into the robust and relatable 37-year-old woman we see today. In a world obsessed with easy labels and ticking boxes, Meghan forged her own identity and has enjoyed the freedom that comes with true self-creation.

For seasoned Royal observers, Meghan's appetite for hard work certainly seems to have left her well prepared. Since meeting Harry, she has dealt with whatever life has thrown at her – be that afternoon tea with the Queen or some very public tensions with her extended American family – with characteristic grace, fortitude and discretion.

This hard-won inner steel has also left Meghan with a strong sense of injustice, and her experience of prejudice goes some way to explaining why she is such a passionate advocate for equality. As Meghan says, her upbringing created, "A social consciousness to do what I could and to, at the very least, speak up when I knew something was wrong."

FOLLOWING HER DREAM INTO ACTING

With a father who worked behind the camera in television, it is perhaps no surprise that the world of acting appealed to Meghan from an early age. But success certainly wasn't overnight, and the aspiring actress paid her dues with a number of unremarkable early roles, including one as "briefcase girl" on the game show *Deal or No Deal* in 2006 – a role Meghan now refers to with some understatement as "a learning experience".

It was only when the then 30-year-old actress landed the lead role of hotshot lawyer Rachel Zane on the successful American drama series *Suits* in 2011

that she was finally catapulted into stardom.

While Meghan may have followed her father's footsteps into show business, she also took inspiration from her mother when it came to the importance of a good education. Doria Ragland earned a BA from Antioch University and went on to be awarded a Master's degree in social work from the University of Southern California, while Meghan herself graduated from Northwestern University in 2003. Indeed, Meghan's double major in theatre and international studies neatly foreshadowed the twin path her career would ultimately take, leveraging acting fame to pursue overseas charity work.

As a college senior Meghan had interned for the United States Embassy in Buenos Aires, Argentina, and, despite her busy TV career, she later became a prominent UN Women's advocate. While very different positions, Meghan said both "helped

[secure] my decision to work on women's political participation and leadership."

This role as both a feminist and humanitarian is one that has continued to flourish as Meghan has stepped up her participation and activism. Perhaps her most notable official role before joining the Royal Family was as a global ambassador for World Vision Canada, which campaigns for better education, food and healthcare for women and children around the world. It was in this role that she travelled to Rwanda for the charity's Clean Water campaign, a trip that she has since described as formative in her passion to make a difference.

She also travelled to India with World Vision in January 2016, in an effort to spotlight the regional stigma around menstrual health for an article for *Time* magazine. This unique mix of globe-trotting travel and good works would prove a perfect finishing school for a modern princess.

TWISTS ON THE ROAD TO TRUE LOVE

A starring role in *Suits* may have brought a useful amount of fame but life was not all plain sailing in this period. In 2011 Meghan entered into what would prove a short marriage with American TV producer Trevor Engelson. The union lasted just two years and, while Meghan has been understandably reluctant to open up about this period in her life, there seems little doubt the entire experience helped shape her views on romance and what makes a lasting marriage.

All of which meant that by the time she was introduced to Prince Harry three years after her divorce, Meghan was a more self-assured, experienced woman, ready to commit to the right man.

Harry met Meghan on a blind date, arranged by a mutual friend in London, in July 2016, when the actress was in town for press interviews for her TV show *Suits*. "I didn't know much about him and so the only thing that I had asked her [the friend] when she said she wanted to set us up was, 'Well, is he nice?'" Meghan later reflected. "Because if he wasn't kind, then it didn't seem like it would make sense."

Harry agreed to the date with a similar level of expectation: "I had never watched *Suits*. I had never heard of Meghan before," he said. Despite this relatively inauspicious start, the couple got to know one another very quickly and it soon became clear that their relationship was serious. As a result Meghan gradually started to distance herself from all Hollywood gossip, including the large social network profile she had assiduously built – with 1.9 million

> ❝ *I'VE NEVER WANTED TO BE A LADY WHO LUNCHES. I'VE ALWAYS WANTED TO BE A WOMAN WHO WORKS. AND THIS TYPE OF WORK IS WHAT FEEDS MY SOUL.* ❞

followers on Instagram and more than 350,000 on Twitter. Finally, in April 2017, in a clear sign that she understood the privacy required of the Royal Family's inner circle, Meghan shut down her "passion project" – her lifestyle website *The Tig*.

It would be another seven months before Harry proposed officially, but the world saw this personal sacrifice as a clear statement that marriage was on the cards.

During its life online *The Tig* had provided Meghan's many fans with invaluable insights into her personal passions, with regular topics including fashion, food and travel, and essays written by the actress herself. In her parting statement posted to the site, the soon-to-be princess succinctly summed up her message to both fans of *The Tig* and all women, "Don't ever forget your worth – as I've told you time and time again: you, my sweet friend, you are enough."

While Meghan was obviously sad to see her site close, she would soon enjoy a much bigger stage to make exactly this kind of empowering statement to women worldwide.

In many ways the stage afforded a Royal is the one Meghan was born for. At the tender age of 11 she watched a commercial played on the television in her classroom that made the dubious claim, "Women all over America are fighting greasy pots and pans". Many years later, Meghan described how her "little freckled face became red with anger" as the boys in her class "yelled out, 'Yeah, that's where women belong. In the kitchen.'"

Incensed, the future feminist leader went home and wrote letters to prominent female figures in America, including civil rights lawyer Gloria Allred and then First Lady Hillary Clinton. Moved by the young girl's outrage, many of these eminent women pledged their support and, a few months later, the commercial was changed to say, "People all over America are fighting greasy pots and pans".

Now that she is a prominent woman herself, Meghan continues to be vocal about "needing a seat at the table". Indeed, if an invitation to that table is not available, Meghan says women "need to create their own table".

Perhaps the high point to date of Meghan's lifelong commitment to gender equality was the standing ovation she received at the UN for a stirring speech she gave on International Women's Day 2015, from an audience including Secretary-General Ban Ki-moon. Commenting on how she combined acting with campaigning, she said, "While my life shifts from refugee camps to red carpets, I choose them both because these worlds can, in fact, co-exist. And for me, they must."

For Meghan then, we can expect total harmony between the glamorous life of a princess and hands-on humanitarian work – after all, it's a juxtaposition she juggled beautifully for most of her acting career. However, the life of a working actress would likely prove much more difficult to integrate and, therefore, shortly before her wedding, Meghan announced she would be retiring from acting to focus on her royal duties, both formal and charitable. "The causes that have been very important to me, I can focus even more energy on," she explained in a statement, "because I think you realise once you have a voice that people are going to listen to, with that comes a lot of responsibility, which I take seriously."

As the Duchess of Sussex, Meghan knows she has been given a unique platform to support the causes that have been close to her heart since her first campaign, aged 11. Addressing global inequality wherever she finds it is how the now-married Meghan really wants to make a difference – and it is perhaps this passion above all that ensures she will make a perfect, and perfectly modern, addition to Britain's Royal Family.

FEMI

NISM

Meghan

FEMINISM

THE MAKING OF A MODERN FEMINIST

From a surprisingly young age, for Meghan the desire to make the world a more just and equal place for women has been a source of inspiration – and action. Her long-held beliefs on equal rights were formed, at least in part, by her upbringing as a mixed-race woman in America, as well as being inspired by both her father and a wide array of empowering women she's encountered or simply admired from afar.

Meghan's stance on women's rights – one shaped long before she met her prince and best outlined in a speech she was invited to give at the United Nations in 2015 – is as clear as it is simple: full equality everywhere. Here are some of the key events in Meghan's journey from precocious activist to global campaigner.

SUMMER 1991
THE SEXIST SOAP AD

Meghan's feminist stirrings found an early expression at the tender age of 11, after her school class was shown an advert for a popular washing-up liquid with the tagline, "Women all over America are fighting greasy pots and pans".

Incensed, the Californian schoolgirl successfully campaigned for manufacturing giants Procter & Gamble, who owned the product, to alter their television advert to refer to "people" rather than "women".

"I don't think it's right for kids to grow up thinking these are things that just mom does," she said at the time. "It's always 'mom does this' and 'mom does that'." In 2015 Meghan reflected on the effect this early crusade had on her, "I remember feeling shocked and angry and also just feeling so hurt. It just wasn't right, and something needed to be done."

FEBRUARY 2015
A TV PLATFORM

Now a famous TV actress, Meghan used an appearance on Larry King's weekly American politics show *Politicking* as an opportunity to outline her own view about how feminism did not preclude femininity. "It's not the F Word," she said of the bad rap that feminism sometimes gets. "I don't think there's anything negative about being a feminist ... No matter what you look like, you should be taken seriously. I think it's really great to be able to be a feminist, and be feminine. To embrace both."

" I THINK IT'S REALLY GREAT TO BE ABLE TO BE A FEMINIST, AND BE FEMININE. TO EMBRACE BOTH. "

MARCH 2015
KEYNOTE SPEECH TO
THE UNITED NATIONS

The then star of hit legal drama *Suits* delivered a widely watched speech to a UN forum on International Women's Day, declaring, "I am proud to be a woman and a feminist." The text of Meghan's speech also noted her concerns for the future, as an activist, "UN Women has defined the year 2030 as the expiration date for gender inequality. And here's what's staggering: the studies show that at the current rate, the elimination of gender inequality won't be possible until 2095. That's another 80 years from now. This has to change."

" I AM PROUD TO BE A WOMAN AND A FEMINIST. "

JUNE 2016
HER PRO-HILLARY STANCE

During the 2016 US Presidential campaign, the popular actress did not shy from declaring her political beliefs. She called the then candidate Donald Trump "misogynistic" and "divisive" and actively advocated voting instead for his Democrat rival Hillary Clinton, posting the hashtag #ImWithHer on her Twitter feed.

JANUARY 2018
OUTING PRINCE HARRY

On a meet-and-greet with supporters on Meghan's first official visit to Wales, a 23-year-old woman told Meghan she was glad there would be a feminist in the Royal Family. "He's a feminist too," Meghan replied, gesturing to Prince Harry.

" RIGHT NOW WITH SO MANY CAMPAIGNS LIKE #METOO AND TIME'S UP, THERE'S NO BETTER TIME TO CONTINUE TO SHINE A LIGHT ON WOMEN FEELING EMPOWERED AND PEOPLE SUPPORTING THEM. "

FEBRUARY 2018
SUPPORTING #METOO

With her wedding mere months away, the future Duchess of Sussex made it clear that her personal politics would not be tidied away, by using a high-profile moment to speak out in support of the #MeToo and Time's Up campaigns against sexual harassment. Meghan was centre stage at an event celebrating the charitable Royal Foundation, and it was her first working engagement with Prince William and Kate Middleton as well as Harry. "Right now with so many campaigns like #MeToo and Time's Up, there's no better time to continue to shine a light on women feeling empowered and people supporting them," she said.

> ## *" IF WE TREATED OURSELVES AS WELL AS WE TREAT OUR BEST FRIEND IT WOULD JUST BE SO MUCH BETTER! "*

MARCH 2018
EMPOWERING YOURSELF

At a Dove Self-Esteem Workshop in Toronto, Meghan spoke at length about self-love and how women need to empower themselves as much as each other. "If we treated ourselves as well as we treat our best friend it would just be so much better! When you see your girlfriends and you hear all this self-shaming and all this criticism, you should just stop and say, 'Hey, that's my friend you're talking about, stop!' And if we did that for ourselves, that alone would create a very different energy."

OCTOBER 2018
CELEBRATING NEW
ZEALAND'S SUFFRAGETTES

Proving she has every intention of remaining an active feminist following her marriage, during her royal tour of Australia, Fiji, Tonga and New Zealand, in October 2018, Meghan gave a passionate speech about women's suffrage at Government House in Wellington, New Zealand's capital city.

Winning over the crowd with a traditional greeting in Maori, the country's native language, Meghan spoke of her admiration of the early suffragettes, who led New Zealand to become the first country in the world to give women the right to vote, becoming a world leader in gender equality in the process.

"Feminism is about fairness," she said. "So bravo New Zealand for championing this right 125 years ago ... we all deeply thank you."

She also read a very apt quote from the most prominent New Zealand suffragette, Kate Wilson Sheppard (1848-1934), who features on the country's $10 bank note, "All that separates, whether of race, class, creed or sex is inhuman and must be overcome."

MAY 2018
A VERY MODERN WEDDING

Meghan's wedding at Windsor Castle was notable for its fresh take on age-old gender roles. In a clear break with tradition the bride gave a speech at the reception, in which she is said to have thanked the Royal Family for welcoming her into it. With her father not in attendance, the independent Meghan notably chose to walk unaccompanied part of the way down the aisle of St George's Chapel. Unsurprisingly the "vow of obedience", which many now perceive to be sexist, was not included in the ceremonial vows and the couple were also pronounced "husband and wife" instead of the outdated, possessive formulation of "man and wife".

SEEKING INSPIRATION: MEGHAN'S STRONG FEMALE ROLE MODELS

Meghan has talked many times, including in an expansive article in the US edition of Glamour *magazine in 2017, about the key female role models that impressed her from an early age – the feminist icons who helped shape who she is, and her beliefs today. Writers, musicians, politicians, even relatives: this group of pioneering women come from all walks of life, but share one thing in common – an ability to lead by example and inspire future generations.*

DORIA RAGLAND, MEGHAN'S MOTHER

Meghan's mum has long been a source of not just love but deep admiration for the Duchess. A trained yoga instructor, Ragland has also done a raft of social work with a special emphasis on helping the geriatric community.

Doria demonstrated to her daughter, from a very early age, the importance of giving back at every opportunity to those less fortunate than ourselves. "Buying turkeys for homeless shelters at Thanksgiving, delivering meals to patients in hospice care, donating any spare change to those asking for it and performing quiet acts of grace – be it a hug, a smile, or a pat on the back to show ones in need that they would be alright. This is what I grew up seeing," Meghan wrote about her mother in a post on *The Tig* in 2016, "so that is what I grew up being."

But good deeds are not all Meghan finds to admire in her mum; she loves Doria's sense of rebellion too. "Mom has always been a free spirit," Meghan recalled in 2016. "She's got dreadlocks and a nose ring. She just ran the LA Marathon. We can just have so much fun together, and yet I'll still find so much solace in her support. That duality coexists the same way it would in a best friend."

MADELEINE ALBRIGHT, US SECRETARY OF STATE

Born in exile in a Jewish ghetto in Prague in 1937, Madeleine Albright made a remarkable ascent to the corridors of power in Washington, where she became the first female United States Secretary of State during the Clinton administration. A prolific public speaker and writer, Albright has been elevated to feminist icon by her eloquent pro-women positions, inspiring a generation of American women including one particular politics student.

"I double-majored with international relations as one of my concentrations at Northwestern," Meghan recalled, "so I've always been drawn to that world. Albright was the first female Secretary of State for the US, the US Ambassador to the UN, an author, and a mom – and she seemingly juggled it all with finesse."

Like Meghan, Albright is a fierce advocate for women supporting one another, having once famously said, "There is a special place in hell for women who do not help other women." Although this was most recently used in reference to women who chose not to vote for Hillary Clinton in the 2016 US Presidential Election, it is in fact a phrase that Albright has used repeatedly over the years.

So fierce is Meghan's own admiration for Bill Clinton's former Secretary of State that she once said, "Put me in a room with Madeleine Albright and, for once in my life, you'll find this girl with the gift of gab unequivocally without words."

HILLARY CLINTON, POLITICIAN

Meghan was a very vocal Hillary Clinton supporter during the 2016 Presidential Election, putting the hashtag #ImWithHer on her Twitter bio. The successful actress admired Hillary's drive and verve, and undoubtedly would have loved to see the first-ever female US President. As Meghan explained at the time of the election, during an interview on *The Nightly Show with Larry Wilmore*, "You're not voting for Hillary just because she's a woman, but because Trump has made it easy to see that you don't really want that kind of world that he's painting."

> *ALBRIGHT WAS THE FIRST FEMALE SECRETARY OF STATE FOR THE US, THE US AMBASSADOR TO THE UN, AN AUTHOR, AND A MOM – AND SHE SEEMINGLY JUGGLED IT ALL WITH FINESSE.*

DIANA, PRINCESS OF WALES

Along with many young people growing up in the 1980s and 1990s, Meghan is said to have greatly admired the late mother of her future husband, Princess Diana, according to Royal biographer, Andrew Morton. It's said Meghan even had a copy of Morton's biography – *Diana: Her True Story* – on the bookshelf in her bedroom. In Morton's telling, Diana impressed the young Meghan for a variety of reasons. "According to family friends, she was intrigued by Diana, not just for her style, but for her independent humanitarian mission, seeing her as a role model," he wrote in *The Sun* newspaper. Although separated by a generation, both Royal brides certainly share an easy charm and winning smile that puts people at ease. And from an early age, Meghan has been involved in the type of charity work Diana performed so well – helping the disenfranchised.

Indeed, now Meghan is an official member of the Royal Family, you can expect the comparisons to Diana to blossom fully. And while Meghan will sadly never meet the woman who would have been her mother-in-law, Harry himself is certain that the pair would get along. "They'd be thick as thieves, without question," he speculated sweetly during the official engagement interview, "and she would be over the moon, jumping up and down, so excited for me."

MISTY COPELAND, BALLERINA

Copeland made history when, in 2015, she became the first African-American principal dancer with the prestigious American Ballet Theatre. Coming from an impoverished upbringing in Los Angeles – when she often didn't know if she and her five siblings would eat that night – Copeland has taken American ballet by storm and become one of the world's most famous dancers.

Meghan, a big ballet fan, interviewed her for *The Tig* in 2014. "As a biracial woman, I know what it's like to want to follow your dreams and hear a lot of No's along the way – not as a reflection of your talent, but because you're just not quite how they envisioned the role," Meghan wrote. "And you may remember my story of being a little girl and wanting a doll that looked like me: Well, Misty is that real life doll – the role model, the pretty princess, the ballerina that the 10-year-old me so desperately needed to see."

DIAN FOSSEY, PRIMATOLOGIST

The famous American conservationist is best known for undertaking an extensive study of mountain gorillas in Rwanda from 1966 until her death in 1985. Fossey actively promoted conservation efforts, strongly opposed poaching and tourism in wildlife habitats, and made the world more aware of gorillas and their plight. She was brutally murdered in her cabin in December 1985, and it has been theorized that her murder was linked to her conservation efforts.

Meghan greatly admires Fossey's bravery and success in saving gorillas – something she got to witness first-hand when she visited Rwanda during her time working for charity World Vision Canada. "I made it my mission to see the mountain gorillas [protected by the Fossey Fund]," Meghan explained. "If it weren't for her, these animals could be extinct."

ROSIE THE RIVETER, WORLD WAR TWO ICON

A stylized drawing representing the many American women who worked in wartime factories and shipyards, "Rosie", as she became known, is a cultural icon of World War Two. Rosie the Riveter appeared on many posters with the catchphrase "We can do it!" and became the subject and title of both a song and a Hollywood movie during the war. Today, Rosie's image is still used to celebrate the thousands of young women who replaced war-bound male conscripts, often taking on completely new jobs, as well as being a feminist symbol of women's post-war economic power.

This strong character certainly wielded her influence over a young Meghan. "Growing up, I had a poster in my room of Rosie flexing her biceps," she later recalled, "and when I was in grade school, I saw this sexist commercial for dish soap. With Rosie's "We can do it!" mantra in mind, I wrote a letter to Procter & Gamble, Hillary Clinton, and *Nick News* anchor Linda Ellerbee, who sent a camera crew to meet me. Guess what? They changed the commercial."

SUHANI JALOTA, ENTREPRENEUR

In 2015, Suhani Jalota spent time with women living in Indian slums. Unable to afford basic sanitary products, the women instead resorted to unhygienic methods, such as old rags and leaves, to manage their periods. Determined to help, Jalota started the Myna Mahila Foundation, a network of women who make and sell women's sanitary products.

Meghan met the Indian businesswoman when she was named a *Glamour* Woman of the Year at a 2016 awards ceremony. Moved by her passion and vision, Meghan later reached out to Jalota and visited her in Mumbai. "I'm incredibly moved by someone who is so eager to help change the lives of others, especially women," she said of Jalota. The pair soon became firm friends, with Jalota attending the royal wedding in May 2018. Indeed, Meghan and Prince Harry chose the Myna Mahila Foundation as one of seven handpicked charities to receive donations in lieu of them receiving wedding gifts.

TONI MORRISON, NOVELIST

A celebrated American writer, Morrison's explorations of the black female experience were honoured with the Nobel Prize for Literature in 1993. Of her own work Morrison has said, "I merged those two words, black and feminist, because I was surrounded by black women who were very tough and who always assumed they had to work and rear children and manage homes."

At college, Meghan elected to take a class on Morrison's works. "The first time I read her book *The Bluest Eye*, I thought, Wow!" Meghan later recalled: "She creates this world for you that you get to feel a part of." The novel, Morrison's debut, tells the tragic story of Pecola Breedlove, a young black girl growing up in Morrison's hometown of Lorain, Ohio.

JONI MITCHELL, SINGER AND SONGWRITER

A vital part of the 1960s American folk scene, Joni Mitchell was a pioneer in the days when men such as Bob Dylan ruled the roost. While Mitchell often claimed to reject the feminist movement, her most famous songs touch on issues that cut to the core of womanhood. As journalist Sheila Weller wrote of Mitchell back in 1970, "Actions speak louder than words – she was one of the major feminist role models of her time."

Meghan, like countless other women, clearly identified with Mitchell, placing the singer in a list for *Glamour* magazine of 10 women who had inspired her. One Mitchell song in particular became a personal anthem for Meghan. "I travel so much for work, press and life that anytime I land back at LAX, Joni Mitchell's 'California' plays in my head," she told *Glamour*, "It's become this anthem of happiness for me whenever I'm feeling homesick."

FINDING HER VOICE
AS A BIRACIAL WOMAN

One important part of her identity, which Meghan says she had to make sense of growing up, is her mixed ethnicity. The daughter of a white father and black mother, Meghan faced both racial uncertainty and explicit racism, making her childhood a challenge at times. Indeed, she once described growing up biracial as "a blurred line that is equal parts staggering and illuminating."

More shocking still was the prejudice Meghan witnessed as a young girl, much of it directed toward her mother. Doria – described by her daughter as "caramel in complexion" – was often assumed by strangers to be Meghan's nanny rather than her mother.

But, by her own account, Meghan's parents worked hard to ensure their daughter was at ease with her mixed-race identity. One Christmas her father even bought two collections of a boxed set of Barbie dolls – one portraying a white family and the other a black

one. Thomas then mixed the two up to show a black mother, white father and one each of the children, and presented it as just one set.

Despite these thoughtful gestures Doria and Thomas were unable to shelter their daughter completely. The sense of confusion Meghan felt at the age of seven when asked to tick an ethnicity box and finding no option for "mixed race" would only grow as she became older and struggled to find her place in the world.

Writing on her old website *The Tig* she explained: "My high school had cliques: the black girls and white girls... Being biracial, I fell somewhere in between. So every day during lunch, I busied myself with meetings... not so that I was more involved, but so that I wouldn't have to eat alone."

A more brutal example of racism was to follow one day when Meghan was home in LA on a break from college. She describes an incident in which her mother was called the "N" word by another driver for not pulling out of a parking space quickly enough. "My skin rushed with heat as I looked to my mom. Her eyes welling with hateful tears," Meghan recalled, "I could only breathe out a whisper of words, 'It's OK, Mommy.'"

Despite desperately wanting to speak up in defence of her mother, Meghan's first instinct was to keep her safe, and so the pair drove away in silence and tears. But it was a moment of injustice that stayed with Meghan for a long time.

On her website in 2015, Meghan wrote a stirring piece entitled "Champions of Change" about the segregation her mother's family suffered during a road trip from Ohio to California in the early 1960s, when her mum was just seven years old. Meghan recounted the story her grandfather told her as a child, describing the young family eating in the parking lot at the back of a Kentucky Fried Chicken because, in those days, people of colour weren't allowed inside.

" YOU CREATE THE IDENTITY YOU WANT FOR YOURSELF, JUST AS MY ANCESTORS DID IN 1865 WHEN THEY WERE GIVEN THEIR FREEDOM WHEN SLAVERY WAS ABOLISHED IN THE UNITED STATES. "

> ## *" WHILE MY MIXED HERITAGE MAY HAVE CREATED A GREY AREA SURROUNDING MY SELF-IDENTIFICATION, I HAVE COME TO EMBRACE THAT. "*

"It reminds me how far we've come and how far we still have to come," Meghan wrote of the episode. "It makes me think of the countless black jokes people have shared in front of me, not realizing I am mixed [race], unaware that I am the ethnically ambiguous fly on the wall."

In the same post Meghan also took the opportunity to thank those who she called "champions of change" – Martin Luther King Jr (p26), Harvey Milk (p27), Gloria Steinem (opposite), Cesar Chavez (below), and her parents for choosing each other not for the "colour of their skin but the content of their character".

As Meghan started out in the acting world, she often found that she was deemed "not black enough" or "not white enough" for a particular role – "leaving me somewhere in the middle as the ethnic chameleon who couldn't book a job," she wrote in *Elle* magazine. It wasn't until *Suits* came along that Meghan found what she later described as her "Goldilocks gig" – a

job that was "just right" and allowed her to embrace her biracial identity.

As a successful adult, Meghan no longer wrestles with feelings of being "other" and sees only the positives of her experience. "While my mixed heritage may have created a grey area surrounding my self-identification, I have come to embrace that. To say who I am, to share where I'm from, to voice my pride in being a strong, confident, mixed-race woman."

Unsurprisingly Meghan feels strongly that people shouldn't be reduced to tick boxes or held back by racist stereotypes. "You create the identity you want for yourself," she says, "just as my ancestors did in 1865 when they were given their freedom when slavery was abolished in the United States."

At no point was this pride in her mixed-race roots more apparent than during the groundbreaking royal wedding celebrations on Saturday, 19 May 2018.

AN HISTORIC MOMENT FOR THE ROYAL FAMILY

When Meghan Markle married Prince Harry, she became the first mixed-race woman to marry into the British Royal Family. It was a pivotal moment for an institution that has long represented – in many minds at least – a certain type of "Britishness" that left little room for ethnic diversity. The significance of this milestone certainly wasn't lost on either the UK's Afro-Caribbean community or for African Americans in the US.

Thankfully, onlookers hoping that this union represented a golden opportunity for race relations were not left disappointed by the day itself. For the ceremony, carefully orchestrated by the happy couple, was an unapologetic celebration of both black and white culture.

In particular, Bishop Michael Curry's energetic and passionate 10-minute sermon about love referenced American slavery and quoted Martin Luther King Jr. The charismatic American's preacher-style speech

resonated with many watching and marked a huge departure from what we've come to expect from traditional royal weddings.

Another highlight was the magnificent gospel choir – The Kingdom Choir – chosen to sing a rousing rendition of "Stand By Me", a 1960s classic which is included in the US Library of Congress as an historical song because of its adoption as an anthem for the black civil rights movement.

In these moments the wedding was elevated to a higher plane, celebrating the entire spectrum of skin colours, not only for the guests present in Windsor Chapel, but for the nearly 2 billion people tuning in across the globe. And the message, crafted in no small part by Meghan herself, of love, acceptance and racial harmony, could not have been clearer on this history-making spring day.

MEGHAN'S LIFE IN BOOKS

Meghan is an avid reader and over the years, in many interviews and in articles she wrote on her former website The Tig, *she has shared some of the inspiring books that have influenced her life. Here is a selection of those titles ...*

THE MOTIVATION MANIFESTO
BY BRENDON BURCHARD

Although written by a man, this fast-paced self-help book is teeming with excellent advice to empower women. The author, high-performance trainer Brendon Burchard, shares how every one of us can reclaim control over our lives by changing the ways we choose to spend our time, money and emotions. Meghan recommended this book for anyone struggling to stay focused on their goals in life, as it reminds us that we're all capable of achieving anything. The only thing standing in our way is ourselves.

WHAT MEGHAN SAYS

"Annoyed by your self-doubt and distractions? The noise that keeps you from reaching your potential? Me too!" She described the book as a "must-have for waking up your inner badass".

THE FOUR AGREEMENTS
BY DON MIGUEL RUIZ

According to author Ruiz, as children we all form self-limiting beliefs that create needless suffering in our lives. This book helps readers understand and utilize "ancient Toltec wisdom" – a belief system of the ancient Latin American civilization – to help them break free from these unhappy beliefs and live their lives with a new freedom and peace. The book proposes a powerful code of conduct to follow, which promises to transform your life, so you can be happier and experience more love. Peppered with common sense wisdom such as "Don't worry what other people think of you" and "Don't let trying to be a perfectionist get in the way of being a good person", this slim volume has become a self-help cult classic.

WHAT MEGHAN SAYS

"My mom gave me a copy of this book when I was 13 years old and, to this day, I constantly circle back to the Don Miguel Ruiz classic for the simplest ways to simplify your life."

THE LITTLE PRINCE
BY ANTOINE DE SAINT-EXUPÉRY

This poignant tale of a pilot and a young prince, stranded together in the desert, has been delighting readers since it was first published in France in 1943, earning it a place as the most translated non-religious book in the world. Ostensibly a children's story, St-Exupéry's tale is in fact a much deeper, philosophical fable examining the human emotions of loneliness, fear and uncertainty – and how they can only be cured by love. It is the character of the Little Fox, who makes a small but vital cameo in the book, that teaches the prince the importance of love. "It is only with the heart that one can see rightly; what is essential is invisible to the eye," he says wisely.

WHAT MEGHAN SAYS

"I have long been obsessed with this book, and specifically with The Little Fox. Even if I don't revisit the entire existential text, the chapter of The Little Fox unearths a truth in me that is always worth the check-in."

THE TAO OF POOH
BY BENJAMIN HOFF

The book is designed as an introduction to the ancient Chinese belief system of Taoism for Westerners and newcomers everywhere. It uses the fictional characters from children's classic *Winnie the Pooh* to explain those in-depth principles in an easy-to-digest and downright fun way. The text provides readers with valuable life lessons such as "how to move in the world" and "let go of stress and sadness". Ultimately, by following the example of Pooh – a bear who is carefree and lives in the moment – we learn how to be happier and worry-free, which is the essence of ancient Taoism.

WHAT MEGHAN SAYS

"Aspects of Taoism told through the characters of Winnie the Pooh *- I mean, does it get better?"*

WHO MOVED MY CHEESE?
BY SPENCER JOHNSON

This classic business book about change is a parable that takes place in a maze where four beings live. Sniff and Scurry are mice, non-analytical and non-judgemental; they just want cheese and are willing to do whatever it takes to get it. Hem and Haw are "little people", mouse-sized humans who have an entirely different relationship with cheese – it's not just sustenance to them, it's their self-image. Their lives and belief systems are built around the cheese they've found. The message contained in the mouse maze metaphor is that we can all start to see change as a positive, rather than a scary, part of life.

WHAT MEGHAN SAYS

"A professor at Northwestern University had this book on our list of required reading for an industrial engineering class I took my junior year of college. It was a seemingly odd choice, but at the end of the day, the takeaway was a self-empowerment and motivational bent that I apply to decision-making in my life to this very day. It's an invaluable quick read."

THE INNER GYM: A 30-DAY WORKOUT FOR STRENGTHENING HAPPINESS
BY LIGHT WATKINS

According to Watkins, the author and Meghan's private meditation teacher, one of the biggest myths in our society is that you can simply choose to be happy whenever you want – even when faced with challenging circumstances. Another myth is that happiness is a byproduct of making more money, falling in love, or being successful. In fact, Watkins argues in his self-help manual, modern research shows that many of our beliefs about happiness are all an illusion. Happiness is not sustained through achievements. Rather, it is the result of having strong "inner" muscles, which you need to learn how to strengthen. Part storybook and part workbook, *The Inner Gym* is broken down into six easy exercises for inner muscles, one per chapter for you to work through, teaching you to meditate as you go.

WHAT MEGHAN SAYS

"A key book for beginner meditation."

WHEN BREATH BECOMES AIR
BY PAUL KALANITHI

A heartbreaking, exquisitely observed memoir that manages to find hope and beauty in the face of a terminal diagnosis, this bestselling book follows an idealistic, young neurosurgeon as he becomes a cancer patient himself. Reflecting on his experiences as both doctor and patient, the ever-eloquent Kalanithi attempts to answer the question, "What makes a life worth living?" Despite being a book about dying, this memoir is remarkably life-affirming.

WHAT MEGHAN DID

She fell in love with this New York Times *bestseller and Pulitzer Prize finalist, sharing it on her Instagram feed as a book to read on long trips.*

GRACE: A MEMOIR
BY GRACE CODDINGTON

This is the fascinating, high-fashion autobiography of a long-serving creative director of US *Vogue*. Abandoning a highly lucrative career as a leading model in London's Swinging Sixties scene, Coddington became a junior fashion editor at *Vogue* where she quickly established herself on the other side of the camera, coordinating photo shoots with the likes of David Bailey, Cecil Beaton and Sarah Moon. Coddington's journey is the inspirational and, at times, incredible life story of a determined, groundbreaking woman.

WHAT MEGHAN DID

Meghan captioned an image of this book "Bedtime stories" on her Instagram feed, signalling it was a book she enjoyed reading.

ELEMENTS OF STYLE
BY ERIN GATES

A uniquely personal and practical decorating guide that shows how designing a home can be an outlet of personal expression and an exercise in self-discovery. Drawing on her 10 years of experience in the interior design industry, Gates combines honest design advice and gorgeous professional photographs and illustrations with personal essays about the lessons she has learned while designing both her own home and her own life. Lesson number one? None of our homes or lives are perfect.

WHAT MEGHAN DID

Meghan shared this design book on her blog, revealing her own love of interior design as well as a strong belief that creating a beautiful home can help nurture a sense of happiness and fulfilment in its own right.

LINDA McCARTNEY: LIFE IN PHOTOGRAPHS
WITH FOREWORD BY ANNIE LEIBOVITZ

This retrospective of Linda McCartney's life and photography is an inspiring book for any women trying to break into a male-dominated field. Linda's career began in 1966 when she snagged a press pass to a promotional event for the Rolling Stones. Her fresh, candid photographs of the band turned out to be far superior to the formal shots taken by their official snapper, securing her reputation as a rock 'n' roll photographer. Two years later, Linda entered the record books as the first female photographer to have her work featured on the cover of *Rolling Stone* magazine, with her portrait of Eric Clapton. She went on to capture many of rock's most important musicians on film, as well as marrying Beatle Paul McCartney.

This picture retrospective is accompanied by an introduction by Annie Leibovitz, another groundbreaking female portrait photographer. Both Linda and Annie are proof that women can break into male-dominated worlds like photography.

IRREVERENT
BY CARINE ROITFELD

This elegant volume is a visual history of the former French *Vogue* editor's fearless career. A daring style innovator, Roitfeld is known for pushing fashion limits with her subversive ideas. Featuring a selection of 250 pages and covers from pivotal editorial shoots and advertising campaigns, this book gives an inside view into Roitfeld's creative thought process and sartorial sensibility. It's a must read for those interested in cutting-edge fashion and femininity, and is a book that should empower women to follow Roitfeld's lead and take risks with their personal style.

WHAT MEGHAN DID

This bold style book was seen on the entrance table of Meghan's home in several images on her Instagram, and style observers have also noticed the Duchess occasionally likes to wear trouser suits evocative of Roitfeld's own signature look.

WHAT MEGHAN DID

Snaps of Meghan's home revealed this book in pride of place. She is also a good friend of Linda's daughter, designer Stella McCartney, who created Meghan's beautiful halter-neck evening wedding gown – and the pair share similar views on ethical fashion production.

FAS

HION

Meghan

FASHION

THE MEGHAN EFFECT

From the moment Meghan Markle's relationship with Prince Harry was confirmed, it became clear that we were watching a style icon in the making. With her effortless sartorial flair from casual to formal, and a strong fashion identity after years as a successful actress, it was also immediately clear to watching retailers that Meghan had the Midas touch when it came to creating demand. Put simply, almost everything she is photographed wearing sells out in a matter of hours.

So desperate are the public to emulate Meghan's classy but attainable look that, within seconds of being snapped in a new outfit, an extraordinary chain reaction is set in motion. Dozens of fashion bloggers compete to be the first to identify every item she is wearing – from her frock to her shoes and earrings – contacting the press offices of designers and retailers across the world to confirm their origin.

As soon as these details are published online, brands from Stella McCartney to Marks & Spencer are bombarded by fashion followers keen to get their hands on a genuine item from Meghan's wardrobe.

The speed and impact is incredible, and very few fashion icons create such enormous surges in sales. With interest on both sides of the

Atlantic, even Meghan's sister-in-law, the Duchess of Cambridge – whose frenzied followers' behaviour led to the creation of the term the "Kate effect" – looks set to be surpassed in style influence.

Kate is reported to add an estimated £150 million to the British fashion industry annually, but in a recent issue of British *Vogue*, editor Edward Enninful declared that Kate's new sister-in-law could eclipse this. "Ms Markle is an astonishing fashion sales force, who is setting the industry alight," he said.

This makes Meghan the most desired female customer of every shop and designer on the planet. "Right now she's at the absolute top," Los Angeles-based celebrity expert and PR Janey Lopaty told *Glamour.com*. "Everyone is watching her. And brands are probably willing to do anything to get in front of her."

Similarly, experienced British PR Jonathan Shalit, who runs the London-based InterTalent agency, told the *Mirror* newspaper, "The Meghan journey has been a completely phenomenal, unique journey. The power of Meghan is quite staggering. I think she could be the biggest fashion brand in the world."

But what is it about Meghan's look that makes her wardrobe so covetable and sends items flying off the shelves? Style commentators believe it's all down to her unique blend of humble roots, Hollywood sparkle – and now a dash of royalty. Meghan's outfits are undoubtedly special but feel everyday wearable at the same time.

Which is probably why it's the casual style choices she makes – the jeans, the flat shoes and simple dresses – rather than the formal hats and dress coats, that create the most frenetic sell outs.

According to John Muscat, founder of Line The Label, the Canadian brand behind the white wrap coat Meghan wore to mark her engagement to Prince Harry, "She always looks like she's not trying."

This effortless chic is certainly something most of us aspire to, but Meghan's spin on more formal wear is equally interesting. Because she hasn't spent her life being groomed for royalty, instead carving out a career as a highly visible actress, her own mature style adds an edginess and subtle irreverence to the classic Royal dress code. It's fresh and it's new.

Some fashion onlookers have also commented that Meghan's outfit choices for notable occasions are a clear nod to the unique style of the late Princess Diana. Certainly Meghan, like Diana before her, understands the importance of conveying subtle messages with a choice of clothing. For example, carefully choosing colours of fabrics which represent or resonate with the place she's visiting or the calendar date being marked. One such occasion was her visit to Dublin in July 2018 when she arrived at the city's airport wearing a deep green sweater and matching shirt by designer Clare Waight Keller for Givenchy – a sartorial nod to the country's national colour.

The two most important women in Harry's life also share a strong sense of personal style and natural grace. But whether Meghan's lasting effect on fashion eclipses the enormous influence of the mother-in-law she never got to meet, only time will tell.

ABOVE: Meghan paired an affordable Marks & Spencer fascinator with an Oscar de la Renta dress to Harry's cousin's wedding.

" *MS MARKLE IS AN ASTONISHING FASHION SALES FORCE, WHO IS SETTING THE INDUSTRY ALIGHT.* "

MARKLE MAGIC: BRANDS THAT HAVE BENEFITED

THE JEANS BY MOTHER

For her first public outing with Prince Harry, at the Invictus Games in September 2017, Meghan wore a pair of blue, distressed Mother jeans. The effect was immediate. "The day after Meghan wore our jeans, we saw nearly a 200 per cent increase in traffic," said the brand's president and cofounder Lela Becker. "More people came to our website that day than they did on Black Friday! There was massive spike for the month of October. We beat our sales forecast by nearly 20 per cent." Interestingly, Mother already had many celebrity followers, including Reese Witherspoon and Gigi Hadid yet, Becker said, "Nothing has come close to the consistent interest in the items Meghan has worn, both from customers and the media alike."

THE MACKAGE DOUBLE-BREASTED COAT

Meghan wore this military-style, navy wool coat by little-known Canadian brand Mackage during her first official engagement with Prince Harry – a World AIDS Day charity event in Nottingham, UK. According to the brand's cofounders, the coat sold out before their team even got to their Montreal office on the morning of 1 December, the same day Markle wore the coat in Nottingham (Montreal is five hours behind London). "The coat sold out within two hours, and immediately we were getting messages asking when we would be restocking it," said the design duo behind the brand, Eran Elfassy and Elisa Dahan. "We saw a huge boost in web traffic."

While the brand immediately started taking preorders on the style for when it was able to restock, within three days they had also run out of the wool used to make the coat. "Meghan had worn that style of coat before, but I was super excited and in shock," Dahan told *Glamour* magazine. "It's not just people in the UK getting excited – it's really a global reach."

"IT'S NOT JUST PEOPLE IN THE UK GETTING EXCITED – IT'S REALLY A GLOBAL REACH. "

THE STRATHBERRY TOTE

At the same World AIDS Day event, for the Terrence Higgins Trust, Meghan matched the Mackage coat with a burgundy-and-blue tote bag from Scottish leather goods firm Strathberry. "Within 11 minutes of photos surfacing, the handbag sold out," Leeanne Hundleby, the brand's PR director told *Glamour* magazine. "Web traffic increased by 5,000 per cent and over 3,000 shoppers signed up for stock updates on the Tricolor Midi Tote."

BELOW: The Strathberry East/West Mini in bottle green, of which Meghan is also a fan.

THE LINE THE LABEL ENGAGEMENT COAT

The white robe wrap-coat from Canadian brand Line The Label, which Meghan wore for the official engagement announcement, crashed the company's website and sold out within 20 minutes of her appearance with Harry at Kensington Palace. "It was insane," said the brand's founder John Muscat. "I did 12 hours straight of TV, phone and email interviews." But the public interest was even greater. "We had 5,000 requests for the coat. It costs £750. That is not something you buy lightly. Requests were flooding in from around the world," Muscat explained. In a clever marketing move, the coat was renamed The Meghan.

THE ENGAGEMENT INTERVIEW
P.A.R.O.S.H. DRESS

The elegant, green fitted dress by Italian brand P.A.R.O.S.H., which Meghan chose to wear for her BBC engagement interview, was out of stock in less than an hour of the interview being aired. "Our e-commerce site crashed," confirmed Marta Maggi of P.A.R.O.S.H. "We restocked it a week later and it sold out again." P.A.R.O.S.H., too, have since renamed this particular style The Meghan.

" THE MEGHAN MARKLE EFFECT IS DEFINITELY REAL. "

THE SENTALER COAT

At the Royal Family's annual Christmas Day church service in Sandringham, Norfolk, in 2017, Meghan wore a smart camel wrap-coat with wide lapels and a belted waist, made by Canadian luxury outerwear brand Sentaler. The £1,000 coat, with signature ribbed sleeves, sold out in 24 hours. "The Meghan Markle effect is definitely real," said Bojana Sentaler, the label's founder and creative director. "Since she wore the wide-collar wrap in camel colour on Christmas Day, the coat sold out instantly and we had an enormous demand for Sentaler that day, as well as for many days after that. We were shipping coats all over the world."

THE SMYTHE COAT

After Meghan wore her oatmeal belted coat by Canadian brand Smythe on a royal walkabout in South London in January 2018, all stocks of the style were gone in six hours. "We reissued it straight away on our website," said Smythe cofounder Andrea Lenczner. "We had orders from places we don't usually get interest – Hong Kong, Scandinavia!"

FROM GLAMOROUS ACTRESS TO ELEGANT DUCHESS

Ever since Meghan stepped into the limelight, the humanitarian and former actress has been scoring style points for her cool yet classic sense of fashion. Her go-to laidback look is clearly influenced by her hometown Los Angeles, with its casual but chic summer-all-year-round vibe.

That's not to say that Meghan's style hasn't changed and matured over the years. In fact, it's possible to clearly chart its gradual progression, as she's honed it bit by bit, until reaching what we would now recognize as her signature look.

For example, between 2007 and 2010, pictures reveal that the then-aspiring actress favoured much sexier evening looks for key events, which often exposed her shoulders and legs. She would frequently wear strapless mini-dresses which showcased flashy details such as metallic sequins or a low neckline.

A clear refinement of this showy style came in 2011, after Meghan landed a starring role as Rachel Zane in the hit TV show *Suits*. Now firmly in the spotlight, Meghan's evening look began to mature as she transitioned to wearing more sophisticated red carpet dresses, with classier silhouettes more befitting the leading lady she had become.

However, at this point the actress admitted to still making fashion faux pas, describing one navy lace Diane Von Furstenberg dress she wore to a USA Network event in 2012 as "too tight, and too short – everything about it was trying too hard."

But by the time Meghan met Harry, with her humanitarian endeavours mixing with her TV work, her style, while still largely casual, was more confident and more sophisticated.

In the months following her wedding in May 2018, Meghan has again shown her capacity to adapt and evolve, stepping up her fashion game once again and really embracing the responsibility of royal style icon.

Indeed, she has already come a long way since the ripped jeans of her Invictus Games appearance, with everything looking just a little more polished and regal.

Befitting her role in royal engagements, Meghan's wardrobe is now notable for longer, smarter coats and dresses with lower hemlines, often finished off for formal occasions with a hat by acclaimed designer Philip Treacy – the go-to hatmaker for the Royal Family.

Some newspapers have claimed that her sister-in-law Kate has helped advise Meghan about royal fashion – not just what protocol is expected but who are the hot British designers worth wearing. It seems likely that sisterly advice has played some role, as Meghan has certainly mirrored some of Kate's formal-wear tricks while still retaining her own unique LA flair.

MEGHAN'S EVOLVING STYLE IN 10 PICTURES

1

SEPTEMBER 2009, AT A PRE-EMMY AWARDS EVENT IN LOS ANGELES, CALIFORNIA

Meghan wore a buttoned-up, black playsuit to this party, teamed with a pair of cream leather thong sandals, a classic Louis Vuitton bag and delicate gold jewellery. This casual ensemble demonstrates that even in her twenties, she favoured a preppie California vibe.

2

JUNE 2012, AT AN EVENT PROMOTING *SUITS* IN NEW YORK CITY

Fast forward three years and Meghan's dreams of landing a big acting job have come true with her winning the role of Rachel Zane in *Suits*, a legal drama on the USA Network. As the show became more popular, so did Meghan. For one of her earliest red carpet appearances the actress looked stunning in this eye-catching, off-the-shoulder little black dress, covered with black sequins. She finished off the glamorous look with metallic heels, a gold box clutch and purple smokey eye make-up.

3
SEPTEMBER 2014, DURING MERCEDES-BENZ FASHION WEEK IN NEW YORK CITY

Sitting front row at American designer Peter Som's Fashion Week show, Meghan chose to wear his design – a striped black and white crop top with an A-line black midi skirt. Around this time, she favoured outfits that revealed a sliver of her midriff and was photographed wearing a few similar-shaped tops. Although chic and stylish, this tummy-flashing shape is unlikely to be something we'll see her repeat now she is a member of the Royal Family.

4
NOVEMBER 2015, FOR THE CFDA/VOGUE FASHION FUND AWARDS IN NEW YORK CITY

Meghan went all out to turn heads in this metallic Misha Nonoo mini blazer dress with a very plunging neckline, teamed with killer black heels and a silver clutch bag. Again, this cleavage-baring look is too daring to be repeated as a member of the Royal Family – but it is a good example of Meghan's earlier sense of fashion daring nonetheless.

5

**JANUARY 2016, AT THE *SUITS*
SEASON 5 PREMIERE AND PRESS
CONFERENCE IN LOS ANGELES**

Proof that even pre-Prince Harry Meghan's
style was starting to become more demure with
age and experience. Here, she pairs a smart and
chic turtleneck sweater with a simple, black silk
A-line midi-skirt. The striking strappy, gladiator-
style heels add a bolder fashion twist to what is
otherwise an elegantly simple ensemble.

6

**SEPTEMBER 2017, AT THE INVICTUS
GAMES, TORONTO, CANADA**

Meghan kept it casual for her first public
appearance with Prince Harry, in a laidback look
comprising distressed Mother jeans, a white shirt
by Misha Nonoo, a brown tote bag and matching
Sarah Flint ballet flats. This is the last time we've
see Meghan's dressed-down Californian style
on such full display, as the soon-to-be-engaged
actress was to quickly embrace a style more
befitting a princess-in-waiting.

7

NOVEMBER 2017, FOR THE ENGAGEMENT ANNOUNCEMENT IN THE GARDENS OF KENSINGTON PALACE, LONDON

Meghan's next public appearance was decidedly more formal, for the official announcement of her engagement to Prince Harry. She wore a white trench coat, by Canadian brand Line The Label, with a dark green dress by Italian label P.A.R.O.S.H., and a pair of nude strappy heels. With the eyes of the world press upon her, the entire look had a classy, corporate-chic feel as if to show Meghan meant business.

8

MARCH 2018, COMMONWEALTH DAY SERVICE, WESTMINSTER ABBEY, LONDON

Meghan certainly wore a royal-looking outfit for her first official event with the Queen, in what many thought was a clear reference to Kate Middleton's formal occasion style. She paired a white coat and navy dress by Amanda Wakeley – a favourite designer with the Royal Family, including Kate – with navy Manolo Blahnik heels. The look was topped off by a custom-made Stephen Jones beret, a demure yet witty response to the royal etiquette of always wearing a hat for official engagements. Meghan also carried a Mulberry bag held like a clutch – again perhaps showing the influence of the Duchess of Cambridge, it long being Kate's go-to handbag style.

9
19 MAY 2018, FOR THE ROYAL WEDDING AT ST GEORGE'S CHAPEL, WINDSOR CASTLE

On her wedding day Meghan, the first woman to be awarded the title Duchess of Sussex, looked radiant and aptly regal in her elegant, bespoke Givenchy gown. Acclaimed British designer Clare Waight Keller – the first female artistic director at the historic French fashion house – designed the dress. The silk dress itself was an understated yet exquisitely feminine floor-length gown, featuring a bateau neckline and a triple-silk organza underskirt.

ABOVE: For her evening wedding reception, Meghan wore a gorgeous floor-length halterneck gown by Stella McCartney.

10
22 MAY 2018, AT THE PRINCE OF WALES' 70TH BIRTHDAY PATRONAGE CELEBRATION, BUCKINGHAM PALACE, LONDON

At her first official appearance following her wedding, the newest member of the Royal Family sported perhaps her most prim and princessy look to date. Again, there is evidence Meghan took fashion notes from her sister-in-law, the Duchess of Cambridge, in choosing a sophisticated dusty pink dress by Goat, one of Kate's all-time favourite brands.

> *MEGHAN CHOSE A SOPHISTICATED DUSTY PINK DRESS BY GOAT, ONE OF KATE'S ALL-TIME FAVOURITE BRANDS.*

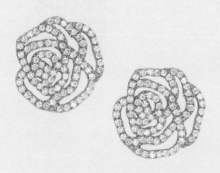

ABOVE: Vanessa Tugendhaft Idylle La Rose earrings in rose gold and diamond.

REGAL AND REFINED: MEGHAN'S BEST POST-WEDDING OUTFITS

Following her May 2018 wedding, the Duchess of Sussex has embraced her new life as a Royal with all the grace and style we've come to expect from the former Hollywood actress. Here, we take a look at some of her sartorial highs ...

LOOKING JUST PEACHY

THE EVENT
TROOPING THE COLOUR, HORSE GUARDS PARADE, LONDON, 9 JUNE 2018

The Queen's annual birthday parade took place on a beautiful, sunny day, befitting the first occasion on which the new Duchess of Sussex joined the entire Royal Family in an official capacity. Meghan certainly looked every inch the natural royal as she waved to the crowds from the balcony of Buckingham Palace after watching the RAF flypast.

THE DRESS

Wearing a pale peach Carolina Herrera top and matching skirt, Meghan's show-stopping outfit featured an off-the-shoulder neckline, oversized buttons and an asymmetric front hem. Much was made by the media about royal protocol usually advising that women keep their shoulders covered. However, with London experiencing a record-breaking heatwave, she can be forgiven for baring a little flesh. Other style commentators noted that it was refreshing to see her pushing back a little against some of the unspoken rules of regal dress code.

THE HAT

Meghan's hat is by the Royals' all-time favourite milliner Philip Treacy. Described by the designer as "a slice with buntal swirls and rosettes". Buntal is a type of straw made from palm trees, while the rosettes were pretty flower shapes crafted from silk satin. The chic headpiece was securely attached with a headband and comb to ensure it stayed put throughout the ceremony.

THE ACCESSORIES

The Duchess carried a pretty, white clutch bag with gold trim, also created by the dress designer Carolina Herrera. She also wore a Birks Iconic Stackable Snowflake ring in 18ct rose gold and diamonds, and the same jeweller's Bee Chic ring in 18ct rose gold and diamonds. Adorning her ears were the pretty Les Plaisirs de Birks Oval Opal earrings, which she had worn when her engagement to Prince Harry was first announced.

FLYING HIGH IN
THE FASHION STAKES

THE EVENT
**ROYAL AIR FORCE ANNIVERSARY,
WESTMINSTER ABBEY, LONDON, 10 JULY 2018**

The Duchess of Sussex looked beautiful as she attended this church service with Harry and several senior members of the Royal Family, including the Queen, to mark the 100th anniversary of the Royal Air Force. It was followed by a reception at Buckingham Palace to meet RAF veterans, serving personnel and their families. The military occasion was a significant milestone in Meghan's public royal duties.

THE DRESS

The Duchess wore a timeless Dior dress in midnight blue, its elegant cut revealing just a sliver of skin along the collarbone, with a boatneck similar in silhouette to the Givenchy gown she wore on her wedding day. The dress was nipped closely at the waist, where it was secured with a skinny belt – very much in keeping with the traditional 1950s shape the French design house first became famous for.

THE ACCESSORIES

Meghan teamed the dress with a chic fascinator by British milliner Stephen Jones, and a simple black clutch and nude heels, both by Dior. The shoes are similar to Dior's classic D-Choc heels – a design by Roger Vivier, who created shoes for Christian Dior from 1953 to 1963. Meghan wore her hair up, showing off her Galanterie de Cartier earrings in white gold with diamonds – a favourite pair we also saw her wear on her wedding day (pictured below).

WHAT A FAIR LADY!

THE EVENT
ROYAL ASCOT HORSE RACE MEETING, ASCOT, SURREY, 19 JUNE 2018

In June 2018 Meghan attended her first Royal Ascot as HRH The Duchess of Sussex. An absolute favourite event of the horse-loving Queen, Ascot is a key fixture in the Royal diary – and a perfect excuse to dress up to the nines.

THE DRESS

For her day at the races Meghan chose an eye-catching black and white hat and a long, cream shirtdress. The frock featured embroidery detail and a handkerchief hemline, and was designed by the creator of Meghan's wedding dress, Clare Waight Keller, for Givenchy. Buttoning up elegantly at the front and cuffs, with a splash of lace detail at the waist, it was impossible for onlookers not to draw comparisons with the Ascot scene in the 1964 film *My Fair Lady*, in which Audrey Hepburn dresses in a similar monochrome palette and hat. And of course Audrey's character in the film, Eliza Doolittle, goes from rags to riches in a Cinderella tale with a twist, which prompted some waggish commentators to note the parallels with Meghan's own life.

THE HAT

The Philip Treacy hat Meghan wore is called the Wave – a two-tone, natural-straw piece, with a turkey feather and patent-leather knot, from the milliner's spring/summer 2018 collection. It's secured to the head using an elastic band and wire ribbing.

THE ACCESSORIES

Meghan wore Givenchy pumps, with a pointed toe and an 8 cm (3¼ in) heel, and carried a Givenchy black satin "minaudière", a hard-sided bag with an ornate clasp and retractable shoulder chain. Her belt was also by Givenchy and displayed the brand's trademark double-G buckle in brass. Meghan chose to finish off the outfit with her Birks Pétale gold and diamond stud earrings.

TRIUMPHANT AT THE TENNIS

THE EVENT
WIMBLEDON LADIES' FINAL, WIMBLEDON, LONDON, 14 JULY 2018

Meghan joined her new sister-in-law, the Duchess of Cambridge, at Wimbledon for the Ladies' Championship Final. Although Meghan is a tennis fan and had been a fixture at Wimbledon in previous years, this marked her first time attending as the Duchess of Sussex. Playing in the final was Meghan's long-time friend Serena Williams, who also attended the royal wedding.

THE SHIRT AND TROUSERS

Meghan looked fresh and sporty in separates from the Ralph Lauren Collection, the brand's most upscale line. Her shirt was the label's Apparel cotton shirt in white and classic blue stripes, and her trousers the Charmain silk wide-leg pant in cream. This modern and slightly masculine outfit demonstrates Meghan's determination to keep putting her own personal style stamp on the outfits she chooses for royal public appearances.

THE ACCESSORIES

Completing the androgynous ensemble, Meghan chose an ivory straw hat with a wide black ribbon, designed by Parisian milliner Maison Michel and called the Virginie. She also sported a pair of Illesteva Leonard sunglasses in matte black acetate. Finally, her matching bag was the Altuzarra Ghianda top-handle mini-bag in navy, from the brand's pre-fall 2017 season, and her heels were the Sarah Flint Perfect Pump 100.

PLEASING PLEATS

THE EVENT
THE MARRIAGE OF CHARLIE VAN STRAUBENZEE AND DAISY JENKS, SURREY, 4 AUGUST 2018

As well as the wedding day of one of Harry's oldest chums, this day also marked Meghan's 37th birthday. The service was at St Mary the Virgin church in Frensham, Surrey.

THE DRESS

Not wanting to outshine the bride, Meghan chose a smart but subtle outfit for the wedding. The birthday look was based around a Club Monaco Shoanah dress in navy, white and green, a style which the retailer describes as having "hundreds of sharp folds and clean, modern colour-blocking". The Shoanah has a v-shaped neckline, three-button front, elastic waist and distinctive pleated skirt. It didn't take long for the Meghan effect to hit – the dress sold out within hours of being photographed on the Duchess.

And it's easy to see why Meghan's followers were so smitten: with its navy shirt top and colourful detailing, this dress is a master of understatement and a modern classic in the making. Meghan herself completed the dress with a Miu Miu knot-tied belt in black nappa leather, from the brand's Autumn/Winter 2018 collection, and wore a previously unseen navy hat by Philip Treacy.

THE ACCESSORIES

Meghan wore her standby black "Deneuve" Bow Pump shoes by Aquazzura, with their distinctive bow at the back. Her bag was the Anna woven straw clutch by KAYU. This California-based ethical fashion brand makes perfect sense for Meghan, with her LA roots and Fairtrade sensibilities. All KAYU bags are made using sustainable methods and materials. Meghan also wore a Shaun Leane Signature bracelet, Vanessa Tugendhaft Parisienne Carrousel earrings, plus a pair of Linda Farrow sunglasses, style 512 C3.

HOW TO DRESS LIKE MEGHAN

Whatever the occasion – be it an official Royal function or informal sporting event – Meghan always looks totally appropriate and effortlessly chic. The Duchess has developed the enviable ability to mix designer pieces with high-street style, and has proved time and again she's not afraid to take a fashion risk.

One reason Meghan can be daring when she wants to is that deep down she knows what suits her, and she has a number of favourite shapes and styles that she repeat buys in different fabrics and wears in different ways. Here are some of the clever style choices that Meghan frequently makes – and how you can apply them to your own wardrobe ...

SAMPLE CINCHED-WAIST DRESSES

A-line frocks that nip in at the waist are a staple part of Meghan's look, such as this simple Jason Wu crepe-back satin, belted wrap dress, worn at the Making a Difference Together charity event in February 2018. A timeless look that can carry you right through the working week to a weekend break in the South of France.

STEAL HER STYLE:

Invest in multiples of this classic shape in block colours, picking sleeveless summer versions in cotton or linen, and long-sleeved winter ones in heavier fabrics such as felt or wool.

" MEGHAN'S SIGNATURE OFF-DUTY STYLE HAS BECOME SYNONYMOUS WITH THE WHITE BUTTONED-DOWN SHIRT. "

STOCK UP ON SIMPLE WHITE SHIRTS

Meghan's signature off-duty style has become synonymous with the white buttoned-down shirt, which helps elevate to chic a simple pair of jeans or wide-legged trousers. This classic example by American brand Misha Nonoo, worn by Meghan at the Invictus Games in September 2017, is a perfect example of the genre.

STEAL HER STYLE:

Shop for well-cut shirts made from pure, good-quality, not-too-thin cotton to guarantee a similarly crisp look.

WEAR SHOES WITH ADDED APPEAL

A self-confessed shoe-aholic, Meghan tends to
stay away from the simple courts and nude wedges
so beloved of Kate, the Duchess of Cambridge.
Instead, she prefers to opt for more flamboyant,
eye-catching footwear with embellishments
aplenty. A good example are the beige stilettos
with intricate criss-cross strap detail at the ankle,
which she wore in November 2017 at Kensington
Palace, following her engagement announcement.

STEAL HER STYLE:

*Look for classic shoes with fancy
buckles, unusual strap shapes or
unexpected details such as bows
at the back of the heel.*

*RIGHT: The velvet texture and leather
trim of Meghan's Jimmy Choo Romy
100 pumps brings an extra dimension
to the classic court shoe.*

" I LOVE THAT FRENCH WAY OF STYLING WHERE IF YOUR OUTFIT IS PULLED TOGETHER, THEN SOMETHING'S GOT TO BE DISHEVELLED – YOUR HAIR, YOUR MAKE-UP. "

BAG SOME CROSSOVER STYLE

For daytime events Meghan tends to choose neat cross-body bags, usually from one of her favourite brands such as Strathberry. But when it comes to eveningwear, she is a fan of the mini clutch. This Gucci Dionysus bag in the supermini size – worn in April 2018 when she attended the Women's Empowerment reception – is adorable. It's practical too, as the chain strap can turn it into Meghan's favoured across-the-body style when she's tired of clutching it.

STEAL HER STYLE:

Choose bags with a cross strap to wear over your body, saving you the hassle of carrying them in your hand. But choose neat, flat designs like Meghan to avoid making an outfit look bulky.

RIGHT: Meghan used the Jimmy Choo J Box clutch at an Anzac Day service.

MASTER THE CLASSY-BUT-MESSY LOOK

Meghan once cited French *Vogue* editor-in-chief Emmanuelle Alt as her style inspiration. "I also love that French way of styling where if your outfit is pulled together, then something's got to be dishevelled – your hair, your makeup," she told *Glamour* magazine. And Meghan even channelled this style philosophy on her wedding day, teaming an exquisite Givenchy dress and flawless make-up with a deliberately "messy" bun.

STEAL HER STYLE:

Pair smart frocks with informal up-dos which leave tendrils of hair falling loose. Or match a beautiful crisp shirt with faded jeans with holes.

INVEST IN A LITTLE BLACK SUIT

Meghan isn't afraid to rock a more androgynous shape from time to time by opting for stylish trouser suits, such as the slender fitted one by Givenchy she wore while watching traditional Gaelic sports on a royal visit to Ireland in July 2018.

STEAL HER STYLE:

Look for a slim, tailored-cut suit. Add a plain white T-shirt or shirt and classic pointed pumps for a sharp, polished look.

PICK LIGHTWEIGHT KNITS TO LAYER

Like so many stylish women Meghan knows the power of a simple classic sweater. On this trip to Belfast in March 2018, she paired her cream coat by Mackage with a chic tonal sweater by Victoria Beckham. Choosing a bright, off-white shade helps make even knitwear feel spring-like.

STEAL HER STYLE:

Shop for sweaters in a rainbow of shades, including black and cream or white. The trick of not looking too bulky in knitwear is to pick very fine knits – lambswool or cashmere are ideal.

BELOW: Meghan frequently wears this Vanessa Tugendhaft infinity ring.

FIND THE PERFECT BLAZER

Meghan has always been aware of how versatile a classic black blazer can really be. In April 2018 she wore this Alexander McQueen version over a green floral Self-Portrait dress for the Invictus Games in London.

STEAL HER STYLE:

Shop around for a really good-quality black blazer. You want a fabric that holds its shape, doesn't crease and is the perfect multi-season mid-weight.

STOCK UP ON WARDROBE BASICS

A black turtleneck may seem like a boring buy but it's a closet essential that pulls multiple outfits together in just the right way. Meghan has a range of turtlenecks in her wardrobe, including this bodysuit version by Wolford Colorado that she wore for an official visit to Nottingham Academy school with Prince Harry in December 2017.

STEAL HER STYLE:

Stock up on this closet classic in neutral shades such as black, white, cream and grey.

LEARN TO SHROBE

Shoulder-robing, otherwise known as "shrobing", is the practice of wearing your jacket over your shoulders rather than having your arms actually through the sleeves. And as fashionistas the world over have been demonstrating for decades, done properly it looks incredibly chic. Meghan is a big fan of the shrobe, which works best with a jacket made of heavier fabric, such as a leather biker or winter coat. Here, she is demonstrating how to shrobe while attending the Commonwealth Youth Forum with Prince Harry in April 2018.

STEAL HER STYLE:

Slip your coat around your shoulders, keep your arms by your side rather than in the holes. Do up a button or two if you fancy – and bingo, you're shrobing!

" I'VE LEARNED TO KEEP THE BALANCE OF THAT CALIFORNIA GIRL AESTHETIC IN A MORE REFINED WAY. "

BALANCE CASUAL AND REFINED

When Meghan started working on *Suits* her style began to evolve. "Being an LA girl, my style was naturally a lot more relaxed when I first started on *Suits*," she explained. But the leading lady quickly learnt how to incorporate a smarter vibe into her signature look. "It still has a casual flair to it but it's a bit more polished," Meghan said of her more mature style. "Whereas I would have normally put on jeans and flip-flops, I'll now put on beautiful flats with my jeans, or a gorgeous heel. I've learned to keep the balance of that California girl aesthetic in a more refined way."

Becoming part of the Royal Family has meant adapting her look again, but Meghan still finds ways to bring a less formal element into the mix, such as with the striped button-front pinafore dress she wore for the Commonwealth Youth Forum in April 2018 – more beach girl than duchess while still remaining elegant.

STEAL HER STYLE:

Stay true to your personal taste in clothes – simply make a few tweaks to smarten or dress down depending on the occasion.

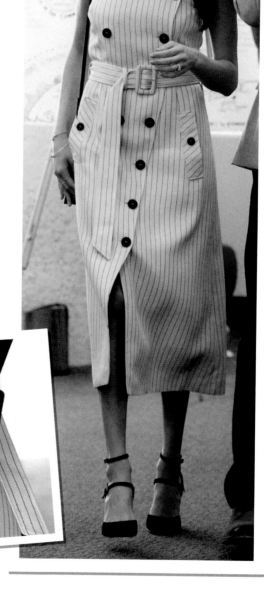

SHOW OFF YOUR BEST ASSET

Meghan has a fabulous figure but her legs are definitely one of her best assets, which means a shorter skirt-length really works on her. Although she has had to pull her hemlines a bit lower since joining the Royal Family, the Duchess still manages to highlight her shapely pins regularly – as seen here in this black Judith & Charles tuxedo dress, worn in August 2018 for a special performance of the musical *Hamilton* in London. She teamed it with a pair of Paul Andrew Pump-It-Up heels.

STEAL HER STYLE:

Whether it's a beautiful décolletage, shapely bottom, honed back or amazing ankles, we all have body parts we think of as our best, and choosing an outfit that highlights these will give you added confidence for that special occasion.

MATCH YOUR ACCESSORIES

Toning accessories make great outfit additions. For example, on Christmas Day 2017 at Sandringham, Meghan matched her hat, gloves, bag and boots in the same shade of deep tan, perfectly complementing her pale putty coat. The unusual cognac shade of her accessories added a rich colour to the overall palette and helped pull the entire outfit together.

STEAL HER STYLE:

Make like Meghan and tie shoes, bags and accessories together in a brighter shade, while keeping the rest of your dress or coat very neutral.

INVEST IN QUALITY PIECES

Meghan knew what she was talking about when she said, "When you invest in a great piece, you're going to pull it out of your closet again and again and put it with a different top or a different sweater. It creates a different, more modern look but it's still the same timeless items." Like her sister-in-law Kate, Meghan isn't afraid to rewear an item on more than one occasion. If she really loves it, the Duchess is also known to buy the same item in different colours, such as the Roland Mouret dress with a waterfall hem, which she has in navy and grey – albeit with different sleeve lengths.

STEAL HER STYLE:

Spend money on classic items in shapes that you know suit you, and in neutral colours so you can wear them again and again.

INVEST IN GREAT COATS

Meghan has no shortage of stunning coats in her
wardrobe, which – as sister-in-law Kate Middleton
knows only too well – is of vital importance when you're
having to attend numerous outdoor events during
the British winter time. For Meghan, the perfect coat
isn't just outerwear, it can be an entire outfit in its own
right. A great example of this is the blue-and-white J.
Crew Tipped Topcoat she wore in Birmingham, UK, for
International Women's Day in March 2018.

STEAL HER STYLE:

*Spend time choosing your coats as they
can really make or break an outfit during
the colder months. Look for well-tailored
structures that have a belted waist to
avoided looking shapeless.*

ADD EXCITEMENT TO PLAIN OUTFITS WITH ACCESSORIES

Meghan knows how to turn a plain dress from forgettable to fabulous with her clever use of eye-catching accessories. For example, here at a World Vision event in Toronto in March 2016, she wears a beautiful pair of very intricately strapped pale heels with an otherwise understated nude dress to great effect.

STEAL HER STYLE:

Be it a pair of skyscraper heels, a "wow" handbag or some show-stopping earrings, invest in statement accessories which can instantly give your outfit the wow factor.

KNOW HOW TO WEAR LEATHER

When it's worn well, leather can look super-luxe as Meghan shows with the now sought-after Mackage Baya burgundy biker jacket she wore to the opening ceremony of the Invictus Games in Toronto in November 2017. Although this jacket is genuine leather, the Duchess, who is on record for shunning fur, has also told how she likes cruelty-free vegan faux leather, which she thinks can look just as good. "Personally, I love cropped pants in vegan leather," she told *Good Housekeeping* magazine.

STEAL HER STYLE:

A very stylish way to wear leather - real or otherwise - is to combine single pieces with softer fabrics. For example, a black leather skirt with a silky blouse, leather trousers with a cashmere sweater, or even a leather jacket and velvet dress.

HEA
BEA

LTH _AND_

UTY

Meghan

HEALTH *AND* BEAUTY

HEALTH AND WELL-BEING

The very picture of good health, Meghan seems to radiate well-being from every pore. Indeed, as regularly documented on her former lifestyle blog The Tig, much of Meghan's time off when working as an actress was spent on healthy pursuits such as baking nutritious food and working out.

And as her love of yoga, meditation and self-help books reveals, Meghan sees nurturing herself on the inside as a vital part of this overall process. Indeed, according to the Californian-born actress-turned-duchess the key to maintaining a healthy work–life balance is focusing on self-love, fitness and mindfulness.

"I think being in shape just means feeling confident, being as healthy as you can," she once told *Shape* magazine. Which means Meghan is no fan of strict weight-watching plans. "I think being happy with your size and being kind to yourself – that's part of being in shape, too. To really just say, 'It's okay if I'm up a little bit this day' or down, whatever it is. Just own where you are and love yourself."

Meghan's healthy habits also seem to have had a good influence on former party-boy Prince Harry, with many friends noting that Meghan has made it

" *JUST OWN WHERE YOU ARE AND LOVE YOURSELF.* "

her mission to try to make Harry healthier. And it seems to have worked. Newspaper reports around the time of the royal wedding commented that the Prince had cut out junk food, started drinking green juices, taken up yoga and pretty much quit smoking.

Indeed, as a former lifestyle blogger Meghan has long strived to inspire others to pursue happier and healthier lives. Here, we reveal some of her favourite fitness and well-being habits.

" *I THINK BEING IN SHAPE JUST MEANS FEELING CONFIDENT, BEING AS HEALTHY AS YOU CAN.* "

YOGA

Meghan's devotion to this ancient Indian stretching discipline is well documented, with the former actress frequently spotted, mat in hand, walking to classes in Toronto when she was filming TV show *Suits* there. "My mom was a yoga instructor so that practice is in my blood," she has explained of her life-long attraction. "I love an intense vinyasa (fast-flowing sequenced) class – and even better if it's blasting hip-hop and done in a dark room with candlelight. The best."

Meghan has said she practices "a lot" of hot yoga – in particular, a form called Moksha which specializes in fast, flowing classes held in temperatures of around 38°C (100°F). This particular type of hot yoga began life in Canada, but has become popular elsewhere around the world, thanks to its combination of traditional stretches with a more relaxed, fun approach. The specially heated room is thought to increase blood flow into the muscles so they're more pliable and less prone to injury, allowing easier movement in and out of positions. Another way in which Moksha yoga differs from other forms of hot yoga is that the room isn't nearly as hot. For example, in the more widely known Bikram yoga room temperatures can reach up to 41°C (105°F). Having the room a few degrees cooler is said to make the practice more comfortable and a little less sweat-inducing.

Apart from her mother, one of Meghan's all-time favourite yoga instructors is Duncan Parviainen, a Canadian who has been teaching yoga since he was 17. Meghan used to attend his classes twice a week during her time living in Canada. She has enthused how Duncan made her "fall in love with my yoga practice... call it a yoga crush at the highest level of Om, if you will."

Parviainen himself is an advocate of Eastern philosophy and the mental and emotional satisfaction yoga can bring. "Yoga always makes me feel better," he said. "On a spiritual level, yoga is my way of connecting with the unseen spirit – a sacred reminder that there is so much more to this life than what the eye can see and the body can touch." As for Meghan, she believes yoga makes her look as good as it makes her feel, and she finds this combination of internal and external benefits pretty compelling. She told beauty website *Gritty Pretty*, "I think that people look their prettiest when they have the yoga glow and no makeup on. Oh my gosh, it's my favorite when all you see is my freckles and my skin and the happiness that I have after my practice."

" *I THINK THAT PEOPLE LOOK THEIR PRETTIEST WHEN THEY HAVE THE YOGA GLOW AND NO MAKEUP ON.* "

KAYLA ITSINES

Although Meghan has long prioritized keeping fit, for her exercise has always been more about physical and mental well-being than the superficial quest for the "perfect" body, which society can push onto women.

As she wrote on *The Tig*, "I had always been of the school of thought that if you want a 'bikini body' you should simply put a bikini on your body." So when Meghan first came across Kayla Itsines, an Australian Instagram fitness trainer known for her "bikini body guides", she initially dismissed it as just "another workout fad showcasing before and after photos of women who transformed their bodies with a regimented programme of cardio, meal plans and resistance training".

But after doing more research, Meghan came to appreciate Itsines' overall philosophy and started

following her workouts for inspiration and motivation. As she admitted on *The Tig*, "Given the insecurities that sometimes plague each of us, having a fitness coach who is equal parts inspiring and forgiving (hey, we're all human – we're not striving for perfect here) – well, that's someone I can get behind."

Itsines now has 7 million Instagram followers, a SWEAT workout app, a bestselling book, and a community of committed fans following her regimes.

As the self-made exercise guru told *Business Insider UK*, "Bikini Body Guides is about the mindset around what bikini body means," she explained. "It isn't this 'sort' of body, it's about the confidence behind it. That's how the programme really took off, and women love it because it was about them getting stronger internally, then externally."

> " *I HAD ALWAYS BEEN OF THE SCHOOL OF THOUGHT THAT IF YOU WANT A 'BIKINI BODY' YOU SHOULD SIMPLY PUT A BIKINI ON YOUR BODY.* "

RUNNING

For Meghan, a self-confessed jogging junkie, pounding the pavements has become a way to stay fit and reduce stress. "Running has always been my form of moving meditation, which I relish because it allows me to get out of my head," she has explained.

But Meghan also acknowledges that running is not for everyone, because the important thing when it comes to regular exercise is finding something that you really love if you want to keep it up. "I love running but I think you have to find a workout routine that really speaks to you beyond trying to get goals for your body," she said in an interview with *Shape* magazine. "For me, running is like,

I need it as much for my head and to clear my head as for keeping in shape."

However, Meghan has also found running can bring out her competitive streak causing her to occasionally overdo it. While the former actress had previously pushed her body too hard, she has come to realize that you don't necessarily have to run far or fast to consider yourself a runner. In a New Year's post on *The Tig* in 2016 she admitted, "If I can't run a marathon, that's okay (I'm getting older – my knees are bothering me.)" As Meghan has discovered, just running for the sake of being in the moment and feeling good can be reward enough.

> " *RUNNING HAS ALWAYS BEEN MY FORM OF MOVING MEDITATION.* "

EXERCISE DVDS

With all the travelling Meghan was obliged to do as an actress and now as a Royal, being able to maintain a fitness routine anywhere in the world is naturally important to her. Thankfully, she doesn't need a personal trainer or a favourite gym to find the motivation or the time to squeeze a session in, which ensures she can always fit exercise into her hectic schedule. "I do it all on my own," she told *Shape* magazine. "I do DVDs at home or I go for a run by myself. I think if you can self-motivate, that's half the battle."

Meghan also confided to the health magazine that she is a big fan of Tracy Anderson, the celebrity trainer best known for working with actress Gwyneth Paltrow. Anderson has created a hugely successful

" I THINK IF YOU CAN SELF-MOTIVATE, THAT'S HALF THE BATTLE. "

online studio, including workout classes which break up exercise into small, manageable chunks, perfect for streaming wherever you are. "I just find the results are great, and you can do little 15-minute increments," Meghan explained. "You just find those little bits of time that help, and then at the end of the day, you've had a full workout."

MEGHAN'S WELL-BEING TRICKS

SET YOURSELF UP WELL FOR THE DAY

" *THE MORNING, AS WE ALL KNOW, IS THAT VITAL TIME THAT SETS THE TONE FOR OUR DAY AHEAD. I LIKE TO PLAY MUSIC FOR A FRESH DOSE OF UNBRIDLED JOY.* " *THE TIG*

DON'T BE TOO STRICT ABOUT FOOD

" *I TRY TO EAT VEGAN DURING THE WEEK AND THEN HAVE A LITTLE BIT MORE FLEXIBILITY WITH WHAT I DIG INTO ON THE WEEKENDS. IT'S ALL ABOUT BALANCE. BECAUSE I WORK OUT THE WAY I DO, I DON'T EVER WANT TO FEEL DEPRIVED. I FEEL THAT THE SECOND YOU DO THAT IS WHEN YOU START TO BINGE ON THINGS. IT'S NOT A DIET, IT'S LIFESTYLE EATING.* " *BEST HEALTH MAGAZINE*

FIND YOUR MOTIVATION

" *MY HEALTH, MY STATE OF MIND, THE FEELING YOU HAVE AFTER A WORKOUT; ALL OF THESE THINGS DRIVE ME TO STEP ONTO MY YOGA MAT OR GO TO THE GYM. SOMETIMES THE IDEA OF WORKING OUT SOUNDS ABSOLUTELY DREADFUL, BUT I ALWAYS REMIND MYSELF OF HOW GOOD IT WILL FEEL AFTERWARD. EUPHORIC, ALMOST.* " *WOMAN'S HEALTH MAGAZINE*

TAKE TIME TO RELAX

" I GIVE MYSELF THE LUXURY OF DOWNTIME. WE ARE ALL SO INCREDIBLY BUSY AND JUGGLING SO MANY THINGS, BUT I ALWAYS TAKE AN HOUR TO JUST DECOMPRESS, WATCH MINDLESS TV, SNUGGLE WITH MY DOGS AND ENJOY A GLASS OF WINE. THAT'S ALL PART OF THE INVESTMENT. IT'S A BALANCE. " WOMAN'S HEALTH MAGAZINE

AND DON'T WORRY ABOUT SAID GLASS OF WINE

" OF COURSE I'M GOING TO HAVE THAT GLASS OF WINE — IT'S DELICIOUS AND I ENJOY IT. DO THE THINGS YOU ENJOY WITHIN REASON. KNOW YOUR BODY AND WHAT WORKS FOR YOU, AND YOU'LL BE FINE. " BEST HEALTH MAGAZINE

BE SURE TO MEDITATE DAILY

" I'M MEDITATING EVERY DAY, TWICE A DAY. IT'S WONDERFUL. ONCE IN THE MORNING FOR 20 MINUTES, ONCE IN THE AFTERNOON. " INSTYLE MAGAZINE

SWEAT IT OUT

" SIT IN AN INFRARED SAUNA AND SWEAT OUT ALL THE TOXINS. THE BENEFITS INCLUDE A MORE SVELTE FIGURE, GLOWING SKIN, AND MAJOR STRESS RELIEF. " THE CHALKBOARD MAGAZINE

BEAUTY

A true natural beauty, Meghan is not a fan of heavy make-up and is well known for her "barely there" approach. The former actress likes to use cosmetics to enhance her beautiful skin tone, dark brown eyes and radiant glow, rather than mask them.

Meghan is dotted with freckles and has often talked about how much she hates it when make-up artists have tried to cover them with thick foundation – or when magazines have tried to Photoshop them out. In a 2017 interview with *Allure* magazine she said, "To this day my pet peeve is when my skin tone is changed and my freckles are airbrushed out of a photo shoot."

According to her favourite make-up artist and close friend Daniel Martin, Meghan has always preferred this less-is-more approach to make-up, and has learnt over the years just how to bring out the best in her natural features.

"She is very easy and just knows her parameters of what she likes and what's she's comfortable in," Martin said in an interview. "We've maybe changed a bit of a tone in the lip or done something different in her eye, but she's very consistent with her makeup."

Indeed, looking at pictures of Meghan as far back as her early twenties, she has rarely strayed from this polished but minimalist look comprised of groomed eyebrows, a little mascara, some natural eyeshadow or eyeliner, a touch of blusher and a nude lipstick or lip gloss. Although she relies on Martin's professional services for special occasions such as her wedding, Meghan, much like her sister-in-law Kate Middleton, frequently chooses to do her own make-up and generally doesn't want to spend a lot of time fiddling around. "She's not a fussy person," Martin has said.

" *EVERYONE LOOKS PRETTIER WITH A SMILE.* "

MEGHAN'S WEDDING LOOK

Despite rumours beforehand that she was going to do her own wedding-day make-up, Kensington Palace confirmed that Meghan's bridal look was, in fact, created by her long-time favourite, Dior celebrity make-up artist Daniel Martin.

For the most photographed day of her life so far, Meghan chose to stick with her signature look: glowing skin, with simple shaded and lined eyes, and subtly glossy nude lips. This classy look perfectly complemented the low, messy bun she chose for a hairstyle. Her natural beauty was enhanced but not exaggerated, with Harry said to have personally thanked Daniel Martin for "making her look like herself".

> " *HARRY WAS SAID TO HAVE PERSONALLY THANKED DANIEL MARTIN FOR 'MAKING HER LOOK LIKE HERSELF'.* "

THE POWER OF PERFECT BROWS

Sherrille Riley, of Nails & Brows Mayfair in London, has helped groom
Meghan's eyebrows in the past and – as you might expect – is a firm
believer in natural brows. For Riley this doesn't have to mean they're
perfectly symmetrical. She doesn't believe you should try and force your
brows into a style that differs greatly from their natural shape. Instead,
she recommends tracing your natural lines and just adding a bit more
colour and depth.

In an interview with *Hello!* Riley revealed Meghan's preferred eyebrow
look is the Audrey brow, named after Hollywood actress Audrey
Hepburn. "With the Audrey, I try to reduce the arch and create a straight
look, but make sure the ends are quite lifted and gradual all the way
through, rather than a tick," Riley explained.

LOOKING AFTER YOUR SKIN

To maintain her beautiful skin Meghan is a fan of regular facials to cleanse, moisturize and boost her circulation. According to a post on *The Tig*, Meghan's mum had talked up the importance of skincare from an early age, telling her, "You must always take care of your skin." By the time she was a teenager this regime included professional treatments. "When I was 13 years old my mom had me start getting facials in my hometown of Los Angeles," Meghan wrote.

These days American facialist Sarah Chapman is said to be the woman behind Meghan's glowing skin. In an interview with *Hello!* Chapman shared a simple extraction regime that she uses when treating clients for pesky blackheads.

The treatment begins by steaming the face to open the pores, then massaging a cleansing balm into the whole face, especially the blemish you want to remove, to help soften it. Then, as Chapman explained, "apply a warm flannel to the affected area and start to apply gentle pressure with a wiggle to either side of the blemish, stopping immediately if you see any blood. It is important to always use your fingers and to avoid using your nails, as this can cause trauma to the skin."

As well as more standard facials Meghan also enjoys pressure-point, lymphatic-drainage facial massages from time to time. These treatments claim to offer an instant tightening and de-puffing by manually draining the lymphatic system, which is said to reduce excess fluids around the eyes and jawline. It is also said they improve blood circulation to the face, giving the skin an instant rosy glow.

FACIAL WORKOUTS

Hailed as a non-invasive alternative to Botox and surgery, Meghan has also talked about practicing facial yoga techniques in her bid to look good and eliminate wrinkles. In an interview with beauty blog *Birchbox* she said, "I do facial exercises from one of my favourite aestheticians, Nichola Joss, who basically has you sculpt your face from the inside out. I swear it works, as silly as you may feel. On the days I do it, my cheekbones and jawline are way more sculpted."

And it seems there is some physiological evidence for such claims. There are approximately 52 muscles in your face, and exercising them is said to release facial tension along with neck and eye strain, according to facial workout fans. The muscles of the face are no different from those in the rest of the body, which means if you don't exercise them, they become weak and flabby and prone to sagging. Working these facial muscles, on the other hand, is said to tone and tighten them and improve blood circulation, delivering important nutrients to the skin, resulting in a clearer, healthier complexion.

In particular, the Duchess is said to be a fan of daily exercises that help release jaw tension. The theory goes that we hold a lot of stress in our jaws, which can lead to soreness, lines and even spot breakouts. By relaxing the jaw muscles we can release this tension, which not only eases pain but also improves skin texture, by helping counteract the wrinkle-triggering grimacing we all do on a daily basis.

SIX SIMPLE ANTI-AGEING FACIAL EXERCISES

Practise these exercises for five to 10 minutes every day, ideally lying down, but while watching TV on the sofa will also work if this helps you find the time to fit it in. Always ensure your hands are clean before touching your face, and remember never to pull or tug on the skin aggressively as this could have the opposite effect and actually accentuate wrinkles over time!

1
SMOOTH OUT YOUR FOREHEAD

Raise your eyebrows in a surprised expression. Stretch them as high as you can. Open your mouth wide, also stretching the eyebrows as much as you can. Widen your eyes a little more if possible. Repeat 10 times.

2
FIRM UP YOUR CHEEKS

Puff out both of your cheeks and shift the air in your mouth from one cheek to the other, 10 times. Then release air while making a small "O". Repeat the exercise 10 times to keep your cheeks firm.

3
SCULPT JAW AND CHEEKBONES

Look up and pucker your mouth like you're about to kiss something. Hold for five seconds and repeat 10 times. For a more prominent jawline and high cheekbones, you can also stick out your tongue while looking up at the ceiling in order to stretch and strengthen the muscles in your neck.

4
PERFECT YOUR POUT

Open your mouth wide. Now, without closing it, make the letter "O". Hold the position for three seconds and do it again. Do this 10 times until you feel comfortable with it and then as many times as you like. Place thumbs underneath your top lip. Pull out gently and at the same time pull back with your jaw muscles. In other words, pull your chin down as though you are stretching your chin line. Do this 10 times.

5
STREAMLINE SAGGY JOWLS

Imagine that you have tasted something bitter like a lemon, pulling your lower cheeks and jawline back away from your mouth. Keep your mouth slightly open and pull the lower half of your face into a grimace or grin. Now try and ignore the cheekbones, only tense the jawline. Do this 10 times. This is great for pulling the jaw muscle back and forward – so long as you feel it stretching, it will tighten any skin that is beginning to sag.

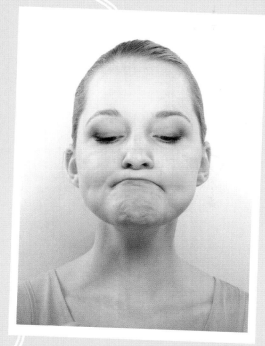

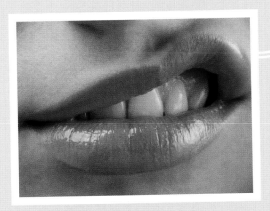

6
REDUCE NOSE-TO-MOUTH LINES

Open your mouth slightly. Now lift your top lip up to the side of your nose (think an Elvis-style sneer). Try it first with both sides and then one at a time. You will find that you will be able to do one side easily, but the other will take a lot more push to get it there.

THE DUCHESS' CROWNING GLORY

It's evident from early photos of Meghan that her hair is naturally very curly – but this is not a look we've seen the Duchess sport in her entire time in the public eye. In fact, ever since her acting days Meghan has undergone regular treatments to straighten her hair. In 2011 she said, "My mom is black and my dad is Dutch and Irish, so the texture of my hair is densely curly. I've been getting Brazilian blowouts for a couple of years."

A Brazilian blow-dry is a semi-permanent straightening treatment in which a mix of keratin – the key structural protein in hair – and formaldehyde is applied to the head to penetrate hair cuticles, smoothing the hair shaft and leaving it straight and shiny. The results can last up to four months, with price points varying from salon to salon and with hair length.

Another, similar method Meghan has used to smooth her locks is known as keratin treatment. Stylist Theonie Kakoulli at Nicky Clarke, where the Duchess has visited, told *People* magazine, "It's great for people with naturally curly hair like Meghan. It takes the frizz out and makes it more manageable — she said it made a real difference."

Like a Brazilian blow-dry, this treatment also involves applying keratin, then using heat to seal it in. However, stylists say that keratin treatments take away even more volume and frizz, calming the curls completely for the ultimate smooth look. This may be why Meghan has begun to favour this treatment since getting together with Prince Harry, as the increase in heavily-photographed public engagements has meant it's vital to keep her hair looking as sleek as possible at all times.

Indeed, the Duchess' new duties may well be behind Meghan's apparent penchant for a low bun hairstyle, as first demonstrated at the royal wedding. Not only is a low bun a very regal and elegant look, it's also very versatile because it lasts all day and works equally well for daytime and evening events. This makes the low bun perfect for royal tours, when Meghan will have a full schedule of events with no time to do a full hair wash and restyle in between. Plus, unlike a ponytail or top-knot, a low, loose bun won't mess up Meghan's hair shape or flatten its volume, which means it can be quickly untied to allow her waves to fall loosely below the shoulders should she want a change for an evening function.

Another thing that's changed about Meghan's hair since the wedding is her hair parting – which eagle-eyed Royal followers have noticed has swapped from side to middle. This small but notable shift again seems to be part of Meghan's transition from Hollywood actress to full Royal. Just as her

clothes have become less casual, Meghan's messier side fringe has given way to a sleeker, straighter centre parting that makes her look instantly more polished. The resulting hair shape frames the face better, making it fuller and more symmetrical and drawing attention to her eyes and smile. It's a more sophisticated, classic look – and all part of the subtle Duchess makeover that Meghan has undergone since joining the Royal Family.

MEGHAN'S MUST-HAVE BEAUTY PRODUCTS

It's no secret that Meghan has flawless skin, but she also knows exactly how to emphasize her natural beauty with a few favourite products that she has come to rely on. Below are the stand-by beauty buys Meghan has happily shared on both her old website and in many interviews over the years.

SKIN

1. CAUDALIE PREMIER CRU ELIXIR

Meghan has said she enjoys using this high-end oil on her skin, which contains anti-ageing grape extract to smooth and soften.

2. TATCHA LUMINOUS DEWY SKIN MIST

According to her former make-up artist, Lydia Sellers, Meghan uses this fine, silky facial spray containing naturally hydrating squalene and red algae extract to
set her make-up and give her skin a dewy finish.

3. TALIKA EYE THERAPY PATCH

Despite travelling constantly and making numerous public appearances, Meghan never looks tired – and these eye patches may be her secret. The Duchess is said to love using these awarding-winning contour strips for 30 minutes around the eye area before going out. They are impregnated with ceramides for moisture and nourishing oils of rose, safflower and avocado to help reduce all trace of fatigue from under the eyes.

4. SANCTUARY SPA THERAPIST'S SECRET FACIAL OIL

Meghan shared on her former blog *The Tig* that she loved to go to the famous Sanctuary Spa while visiting London. This luxury, women-only pampering spot was a British institution, founded in 1977 as a secret space where ballerinas from the nearby Royal Opera House could relax and be pampered between gruelling shows. One of Meghan's favourite products from the Sanctuary's in-house range is said to be their facial oil. It contains a blend of rosehip, sunflower, jojoba, wheatgerm, frankincense and rose oils to plump skin and leave it with a youthful glow.

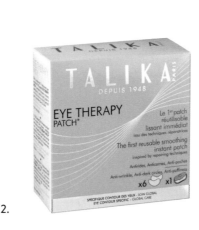

1.   2.   3.   4.

1.   2.   3.   4.

MAKE-UP

1. LAURA MERCIER FOUNDATION PRIMER

"I don't wear foundation unless I'm filming, so this is what I put on every day after moisturizer to give my skin a dewy glow," Meghan told *Today* magazine. The primer is designed to provide the skin with a sheer, healthy glow, creating an incredibly smooth, natural-looking complexion.

2. CHANEL SUBLIMAGE LE TEINT ULTIMATE RADIANCE-GENERATING CREAM FOUNDATION

On the occasions when she does wear full foundation, this is one of Meghan's go-tos, providing good coverage without hiding her best features. "I never want to cover my freckles, so we just do a 'wash' of foundation in certain sections instead of over the entire face," she told *Birchbox*. As well as providing moisturizing, all-day cover, this pricey foundation from Chanel contains luxury ingredients such as diamond powder, to give skin a luminous finish.

3. MAC EYELINER

Recommended to her by make-up artist Kayleen McAdams, Meghan is said to be a huge fan of this eyeliner in Teddy, a brown shade with a hint of gold that makes her dark eyes really pop. Kayleen apparently also used Teddy when making up Sofia Vergara, the star of sitcom *Modern Family* and noted Colombian beauty, a fact that was recommendation enough for Meghan. "Sofia Vergara? Who wouldn't want those gorgeous brown almond eyes?" the Duchess asked rhetorically.

4. DIORSHOW ICONIC MASCARA

Meghan's eyes are certainly one of her best features, and in order to accentuate them, she swears by this luxurious mascara that adds volume and intense definition to her lashes.

5.

6.

5. REVITALASH

This cult growth serum contains a cocktail of peptides and botanical extracts to help strengthen, condition and enhance your natural lashes. "I swear they are as long as they could ever be," Meghan told *Allure* magazine after using it.

6. MAKE UP FOR EVER HD POWDER

This super-fine, loose finishing powder helps smooth the overall look of the skin as well as minimize pores, and is described as "a veil to matte-ify and blur your complexion". Meghan is a fan, telling *Allure*, "It lets your skin look shiny and fresh, but not greasy-shiny."

7. NARS ORGASM BLUSH

This bestselling blush is loved for its soft pink glow and hint of shimmer, and is another essential in Meghan's make-up bag. "It's a perfect, rosy flush tone that brightens the face," she told *Beauty Banter*.

8. YVES SAINT LAURENT TOUCHE ÉCLAT CONCEALER

Loved by make-up artists for its ability to instantly brighten under eyes, this is another of Meghan's favourites.

7.

8.

LIPS

1. CYNTHIA ROWLEY VALENTINE CREAMY LIP STAIN

This pretty lip stain is used by Meghan and mentioned on her former blog. It gives beautifully smooth lips with just a hint of natural colour.

2. CHARLOTTE TILBURY MATTE REVOLUTION LIPSTICK IN VERY VICTORIA

The celebrated British brand, created by celebrity make-up artist Charlotte Tilbury, makes one of Meghan's favourite lipsticks, according to *Hello!* magazine. Her preferred shade is apparently "Very Victoria" – a gorgeous taupe-nude matte that the Duchess is said to have worn for her engagement day photos.

3. FRESH SUGAR ADVANCED THERAPY LIP TREATMENT WITH SPF 15

This ultra-nourishing lip treatment promises to significantly boost moisture, enhance volume and improve the definition of the lip area – and Meghan is certainly a fan. "I have searched high and low and tried every kind of lip balm but this is the very best," she said about this product. "Soft, kissable, buttery lips. I swear by it."

1.

2.

3.

NAILS

1. ESSIE BALLET SLIPPERS NAIL POLISH

A Royal favourite also used by both the Queen and the Duchess of Cambridge, Meghan chose to wear this nail varnish on her wedding day to Prince Harry – and has worn the natural but polished pale pink shade several times since.

2. RIMMEL LONDON SUPER GEL POLISH IN IVORY TOWER

You never see Royals with coloured nails – it's neutral all the way. And this is another incredibly natural and flattering shade, which Meghan has worn on several public occasions. This polish has the added bonus of lasting for up to 10 days without chipping.

1. 2.

BODY

1. DR BRONNER'S LANDER PURE-CASTILE LIQUID SOAP

First created in 1948, Dr Bronner soaps are famed for their organic ingredients and velvety lather, which leave skin clean and silky smooth. "I love the [lavender] smell and it lasts for such a long time," Meghan has said. "The almond scent is quite nice too if you prefer something warm and sweet. I alternate between the two."

2. NIVEA SKIN FIRMING HYDRATION BODY LOTION

Meghan says this very affordable moisturizer makes her skin look and feel amazing. "I would buy a case of this at a time if I could find it," she has said. The secret ingredient is Coenzyme Q10, a natural component of healthy skin, which actively works to keep it soft, toned and supple.

3. DECLÉOR AROMA NUTRITION NOURISHING RICH BODY CREAM

For a more pampering, treat Meghan is said to enjoy the smooth, melting texture and delicate fragrance of this rich body cream. It promises to intensely nourish the skin, leaving it feeling smoother and more comfortable.

1. 2. 3.

FRAGRANCE

1. BVLGARI BLV II EAU DE PARFUM

Meghan has often talked of her love of this scent, which is described as an "elegant floral with citrusy, spicy and woody undertones".

2. ORIBE CÔTE D'AZUR EAU DE PARFUM

Another Meghan pick, this scent is said to embody the glamour and heat of the legendary French resort it's named after, containing sun-drenched notes of bergamot, jasmine and sandalwood.

3. JO MALONE WOOD SAGE AND SEA SALT COLOGNE

The former actress has said she adores this fresh fragrance from the celebrated British brand, which combines the scent of sea air mingled with herbal sage.

1.   2.   3.

HAIR

1. WELLA OIL REFLECTIONS LUMINOUS SMOOTHENING OIL

Harnessing camellia oil and white tea extract, this oil infuses hair with long-lasting moisture and provides a mirror-like shine from root to tip. It can be used as a styling product, leave-in treatment or pre-shampoo oil. Meghan is a big fan of its flexibility, telling the blog *Beauty Banter*, "It smells like vacation and makes your hair slippery and touchable. I love this stuff! It also doubles as a pretty amazing body oil post-bath."

2. KÉRASTASE OLEO-RELAX ANTI-FRIZZ MASQUE

Meghan swears by this hair mask, using it when her hair needs an intensive moisture boost. It's packed with nourishing ingredients, including natural oils and silicone, and is designed to tame dry and rebellious hair and help achieve a smooth, healthy look.

1.   2.

FO

OD

Meghan

FOOD

———

MEGHAN'S LOVE OF ALL THINGS CULINARY

Meghan is a self-confessed foodie who adores both creating delicious dishes in the kitchen and eating out at some of the world's hottest restaurants. Unsurprisingly, food played an integral role on her former lifestyle blog The Tig. *Indeed, the tagline at the bottom of each page described the site as "a hub for the discerning palate – those with a hunger for food, travel, fashion, and beauty". And those same pages were frequently packed with recipes for tasty-sounding treats and interviews with inspiring chefs.*

For Meghan, then, food is so much more than just fuel; it also represents family, home and love. In an interview with Athena Calderone, from the food and design blog *EyeSwoon*, Meghan explained that her love of cooking started in childhood, when she first learned "how connective food could be – how happy people would be when I walked in with a tray of perfect crudités".

To this day Meghan uses the social side of eating as a way to reconnect with people and to boost her own mood, along with that of her loved ones. "I am a big fan of Sunday suppers," she admitted to TV show *Today*. "Whether we're eating lamb tagine, pot roast or a hearty soup, the idea of gathering for a hearty meal with friends and family on a Sunday makes me feel comforted."

Always a true Californian girl at heart, in recent years Meghan has focused more on sustainable

foods and a healthy eating ethos, while always maintaining a sense of balance and an everything-in-moderation approach. Which means the Duchess will happily enjoy an occasional indulgence like French fries or pasta carbonara, but day to day she tends to eat fresh, nutritious foods such as smoothies and sushi, and keeps herself hydrated by sipping hot water with lemon. While filming her TV show *Suits*, Meghan tended to follow a vegan diet during the week, then eat much less rigidly at weekends.

But as well as monitoring the nutritional value of what she is eating, choosing the right taste and flavour combinations is just as vital to Meghan, as many of the recipes she shared on *The Tig* reveal. All of her favourite recipes centre around fresh ingredients and bold flavours and can easily be replicated at home.

" THE IDEA OF GATHERING FOR A HEARTY MEAL WITH FRIENDS AND FAMILY ON A SUNDAY MAKES ME FEEL COMFORTED. "

10 RECIPES INSPIRED BY MEGHAN'S FAVOURITES

COCONUT AND BERRY SMOOTHIE

Meghan shared the recipe for her favourite breakfast smoothie – packed with energizing, healthy ingredients – in an interview with *The Chalkboard* in 2015. According to Meghan, sometimes she likes to mix the smoothie recipe up by using "frozen mango, a squeeze of lime". Here is a similar energy-boosting smoothie to try.

INGREDIENTS

50 g (¼ cup) frozen mixed berries
1 tsp coconut oil
50 g (¼ cup) cashew nuts
125 ml (½ cup) almond milk
125 ml (½ cup) coconut water
Handful of coconut shavings and chocolate (optional)

TO MAKE:

Blitz together in a blender or Nutribullet. Top with coconut shavings and, if you feel like a treat, drizzle with chocolate.

MEDITERRANEAN-STYLE KALE SALAD

When Meghan shared a tasty salad recipe packed with traditional Greek flavours on her blog, she talked about how she, like many people, had become fed up with the healthy obsession for kale with everything. But she then insisted that after trying one particular salad – first developed by Anastasia Koutsioukis and Ahmet Erkaya of Mandolin Aegean Bistro, Miami, a Mediterranean restaurant – her faith in kale was "restored". And of the talented chefs behind the idea, she said, "The dynamic duo has a taste level that makes their concept and dishes irresistible." Here is a salad recipe inspired by similar flavours.

INGREDIENTS

1 bag of kale
1/2 red onion, chopped
40 g (1/3 cup) chopped walnuts
40 g (1/3 cup) cherry tomatoes, halved
50 g (1/2 cup) shaved Parmesan cheese

FOR THE DRESSING

2 tbsp extra virgin olive oil
1/2 lemon, juiced
1 tsp honey
1 tbsp balsamic vinegar
1/2 tsp chilli flakes
Sea salt and freshly ground pepper to taste

Serves 4

TO MAKE:

1   *Wash the kale and remove the stems, then slice, along with the red onion and cherry tomatoes.*
2   *Whisk together all the ingredients for the dressing.*
3   *Add the vegetables to the dressing and toss together.*
4   *In a dry pan, toast walnuts gently for two or three minutes.*
5   *To serve: Mix the nuts with the salad thoroughly and top with the Parmesan shavings.*

FRESH PASTA

Even with her impressive cookery credentials, when it came to making pasta from scratch, like many of us, Meghan admitted she felt pretty daunted at the thought. But she didn't let that stop her. "I decided to get over myself, and dive right in," she told her blog followers. The former actress described the successful results as a "magical unctuous pasta that made this meal not just a dinner, but a stamp in my passport." But if you don't want to make your own pasta, this traditional sauce can be added to the shop-bought variety for a tasty Meghan-style supper. Serves four.

INGREDIENTS FOR THE DOUGH

450 g (3 cups) 00 pasta flour
3 large eggs
2 egg yolks

TO MAKE:

1 *Make a mound out of the flour on your kitchen counter.*
2 *Make a well in the centre of the mound.*
3 *Break in the eggs and egg yolks, and beat them together with a fork, beginning to incorporate the flour bit by bit.*
4 *Once around half of the flour is incorporated, use your fingers to incorporate the rest of the flour, bringing the mix together into a rough dough. If you need to, add more egg yolk or a sprinkling of water until all the flour is absorbed into the dough.*
5 *Knead the dough until it feels soft and silky, which will take about five minutes.*
6 *Wrap your dough up in kitchen wrap and refrigerate for at least half an hour.*
7 *Dust your kitchen counter with some more 00 flour so your dough doesn't stick to the surface, then take a lump of dough about the size of a fist and flatten it with your fingers.*
8 *Run the dough through the rollers of your pasta machine, then fold it, sprinkle with flour and roll it through again. Repeat until your pasta is silky and smooth, and thin enough to see your hand through.*
9 *Run your pasta through the cutting attachment of your machine at the desired setting. Arrange the finished pasta into nests and cover until you are ready to cook.*

INGREDIENTS FOR THE SAUCE

½ onion, chopped
3 cloves of garlic, chopped
2 tbsp olive oil
1 rasher of chopped bacon or a handful of chopped pancetta
1 pinch of dried chilli
1 can of chopped tomatoes
Handful of fresh basil to serve

TO MAKE:

1 *Heat the olive oil in a pan, add the onion and bacon and cook for a few minutes until translucent but not browned. Add the garlic and pinch of chilli and sauté for a few minutes, until the aroma is released.*
2 *Add the tomatoes and simmer for 30 minutes.*
3 *Serve with al dente pasta, adding torn basil leaves and a little grated Parmesan cheese on top.*

PERFECT ROAST CHICKEN

Food clearly plays an important role in Meghan's relationships and she revealed that Prince Harry got down on one knee to propose while the couple were at home making roast chicken. It's now widely assumed that the recipe she followed was this favourite one she'd talked about before. "There is nothing as delicious (or as impressive) as a perfectly roasted chicken," Meghan once told *Good Housekeeping*. "And if you have an Ina Garten-level roasted-chicken recipe, it's a game changer," she said of this recipe. "I bring that to dinner parties and make a lot of friends." Indeed, following the engagement announcement, Ina Garten – celebrity chef and host of *Barefoot Contessa* on the Food Network – tweeted, "Congratulations to Prince Harry and Meghan! I always knew roast chicken had magic powers!! I'm so happy for both of you!" Here is an easy, classic roast chicken recipe to try.

INGREDIENTS

1 large free-range chicken
1 lemon, halved
Small handful of garlic cloves
Bunch of fresh rosemary
2 tbsp olive oil
Sea salt and freshly ground black pepper
250 ml (1 cup) Chicken stock
1 tbsp plain flour

TO MAKE:

1 *Preheat the oven to 200°C (gas mark 6).*
2 *Place the chicken in a large roasting pan and stuff with the bunch of rosemary, both halves of the lemon, and the garlic cloves. Brush the chicken skin with the olive oil and sprinkle liberally with salt and pepper.*
3 *Roast for 1–1½ hours, or until the juices run clear when you cut between the leg and the breast.*
4 *Remove the chicken from the pan and rest on a serving platter while you make the gravy.*
5 *To make the gravy, skim and remove the fat from the surface of the pan juices, leaving about 1½ tablespoons of fat in the pan. Place the pan over a medium heat. Remove the lemon and garlic from inside the chicken and add to the pan, squashing them with a wooden spoon to release their juices.*
6 *Add the flour and stir together with the juices to make a paste. Stir for a minute or two, then gradually pour in the stock, still stirring, until you have a smooth sauce. Simmer until you are happy with the thickness of the sauce, then strain and serve with slices of the chicken, roast or mashed potatoes and greens.*

CACIO E PEPE

When she was asked by Athena Calderone from the blog *EyeSwoon* in 2015, "What is your go-to recipe you make with your eyes closed?" Meghan immediately replied, "Cacio e Pepe pasta... so easy." This Italian classic contains just three ingredients and takes only 10–15 minutes to whip up, yet tastes sophisticated and authentic. Here's a simple recipe to try.

INGREDIENTS

200 g (7oz) spaghetti
1 tsp freshly cracked black pepper
80 g (3 oz) finely grated Pecorino Romano cheese

Serves 2

TO MAKE:

1 *Bring a large pan of water to the boil. Season with salt; add pasta and cook, stirring occasionally, until about 2 minutes before tender. Drain, reserving 175 ml (¾ cup) of pasta cooking water.*

2 *Add 125 ml (½ cup) reserved pasta water to the pan and bring to a simmer. Then add the cooked pasta and reduce heat to low. Add the Pecorino and black pepper, stirring and tossing with tongs vigorously until the cheese is melted and the sauce coats every strand of the pasta.*

3 *Transfer the pasta to warm bowls and serve, with a little more pepper over the top.*

BARBECUED SPICY PRAWN SALAD

Meghan appeared in a video clip for the food channel on the *Today* website cooking a tasty prawn dish over an outdoor barbecue. The delicious but healthy meal combined lettuce salad with spicy grilled prawns, for a tasty but light summer meal. This similar version is just as healthy and delicious.

INGREDIENTS

400 g (14 oz) raw, shelled king prawns
3 tbsp lemon juice
1 tbsp Cajun spice mix
1 tbsp olive oil
4 wooden or metal skewers
1 lettuce
½ red onion, chopped
10 cherry tomatoes, halved
30 g (1 oz) Parmesan cheese, shaved

FOR THE DRESSING

2 tbsp olive oil
1 tbsp balsamic vinegar
1 tsp Dijon mustard

Serves 4

TO MAKE:

1 *Combine the Cajun spice mix, lemon juice and olive oil in a bowl. Add the prawns and stir, ensuring they are coated well with the spice mix. Then, thread the prawns onto the skewers.*
2 *To make the salad, wash and shred the lettuce and mix with the red onion and tomatoes. Mix all the dressing ingredients together in a jam jar and shake to combine. Pour over the salad and toss together.*
3 *Grill the skewered prawns over a barbecue – or under your oven grill – for 5-7 minutes until cooked through.*
7 *Top the salad with the grilled prawns and some Parmesan shavings.*

BAKED EGGS IN AVOCADO

Meghan has described eggs with avocado as "the perfect brekkie". Not only are they easy to make, she pointed out on *The Tig*, they are also, "packed with good fats, omegas, protein and mad flavor". Impress your brunch guests with this simple recipe.

INGREDIENTS

2 avocados
4 eggs
Greek yoghurt, sea salt, chopped parsley and chilli flakes to serve

Serves 2

TO MAKE:

1 Preheat the oven to 220°C (gas 7).
2 Cut your avocado in half lengthways and remove the stone, scooping out enough of the fresh to fit an egg into each half.
3 Lie the avocados in a small baking tray and crack an egg into each avocado half.
4 Bake in the oven for 10-15 minutes, or until the egg white is opaque and set.
5 Serve with a dollop of Greek yoghurt, and sprinkle with sea salt, chopped parsley and chilli flakes.

ZUCCHINI BOLOGNESE

Meghan shared her love for courgette pasta sauce with food blog Delish, which she claims tastes delicious while being amazingly healthy too. "The sauce gets so creamy, you'd swear there's tons of butter and oil in it, but it's just zucchini (courgette), water, and a little bouillon," Meghan said. According to the same interview in Delish, the idea first came about when a friend convinced her to slow-cook courgette for four to five hours, until it breaks down into what the former actress described as a "filthy, sexy mush." Here is a Meghan-inspired version of courgette-based pasta sauce.

INGREDIENTS

1 tbsp olive oil
2 garlic cloves, finely chopped
½ chopped onion
600 g (20 oz) courgettes, sliced
1 tbsp lemon juice
1 tbsp crème fraîche
Salt and pepper
Grated Parmesan and chilli flakes to serve

Serves 4

TO MAKE:

1 *Heat the olive oil on a medium heat with the onion and garlic for about five minutes, until the onion is softened.*
2 *Add the sliced courgettes and cook on a low heat for up to an hour until they are completely soft and broken down. Stir regularly to prevent sticking to the bottom, adding a splash of water if needed.*
3 *Meanwhile, cook the pasta of your choice.*
4 *Remove the courgettes from the heat and season with the lemon, salt and pepper and stir in the crème fraîche.*
5 *Serve the sauce with the pasta, a drizzle of extra virgin olive oil, some grated Parmesan and a pinch of chilli.*

CHOCOLATE FONDANTS

Although Meghan enjoys most cooking, in order to put in the extra effort it requires to bake cakes, she told followers of her former blog that the result had to be "soul-satisfying, like a good hug on a bad day" and "taste unquestionably delicious". With that in mind she shared an indulgent but easy recipe for chocolate fondant, with a gooey center, describing it as "a no-brainer". This similar version of the dessert is easy to follow and delicious.

INGREDIENTS

150 g (5 oz) good quality dark chocolate

85 g (²/₃ cup) caster sugar

150 g (³/₄ cup) butter, chopped, plus extra for greasing

2 tbsp plain flour

3 whole eggs

4 egg yolks

Cream or ice cream to serve

4 ramekins

Serves 4

TO MAKE:

1 Grease the ramekins with a little butter, line with baking parchment and chill in the fridge for at least 30 minutes. Preheat the oven to 180°C (gas mark 4).

2 Melt the butter and the chocolate gently together in a heatproof bowl over a pan of simmering water until combined. Remove from heat.

3 Whisk the eggs, egg yolks and sugar together in a mixing bowl until light and fluffy.

4 Fold the flour and chocolate into the egg mixture and combine.

5 Pour the mixture into the buttered ramekins.

6 Cook in the oven for 7 to 8 minutes or until the edges are set and the middle is still soft.

7 Allow to rest for 2 minutes, then carefully turn out onto serving plates.

8 Serve immediately with cream or ice cream.

MEGHAN'S WINTER BERRY PORRIDGE

Billed as the perfect winter warming breakfast, Meghan shared what she described as a "delectable rendition of classic oatmeal made fanciful with the addition of a brûlée topping". She suggested topping a warm bowlful of porridge with fresh berries for a "special start to the day". Here's a similar recipe.

INGREDIENTS

160 g (1 ²/₃ cups) porridge oats
600 ml (2 ¹/₂ cups) of dairy milk, almond or oat milk
1 tbsp maple syrup
1 grated apple
Small handful of mixed seeds
30 g (¹/₄ cup) raisins
30 g (¹/₄ cup) chopped almonds

1 tsp cinnamon
Handful of mixed berries
More fresh berries to serve and some Greek yoghurt

Serves 2

TO MAKE:

1 Gently heat the oats, milk and cinnamon in a small non-stick pan. Bring to a steady simmer.
2 Cook for 5 minutes, stirring often to prevent sticking. Add additional milk if the porridge becomes too thick or dry.
3 Remove from the heat and mix in the maple syrup, seeds, nut, dried fruit and fresh fruit.
4 Serve in bowls topped with a dollop of Greek yoghurt, a sprinkling of cinnamon and some fresh berries.

MEGHAN'S SIX FAVOURITE SUPERFOODS

As a self-proclaimed health food enthusiast, Meghan has often talked about her love of vegan food. But while the LA trendsetter sticks to a pretty healthy diet most of the time, she doesn't believe in banning any foods. "I think if you deprive yourself of anything you're just going to crave it more, so for me it's just finding that balance," she once told Shape Magazine.

Here are some of the Duchess's favourite foods – and why they're so good for you.

AÇAI BOWL

Meghan has stated in the past that a healthy açai bowl is one of her go-to breakfasts. An açai bowl is basically a thick smoothie eaten with a spoon, which blends puréed açai berries – a trendy superfood – with milk and other healthy ingredients, such as bananas and blueberries, until creamy.

On New York-based lifestyle blog, *EyeSwoon*, Meghan shared a photo of her favourite açai bowl recipe, which blends bananas and berries with almond milk and manuka honey, topped with fresh berries, banana slices, coconut flakes and bee pollen.

WHY IT'S GOOD FOR YOU:

Packed with vitamins, antioxidants, protein and fibre, a bowl of açai and fruity friends is a really nutritious start to the day that will give you heaps of energy and also keep you feeling fuller for longer so you're less likely to snack.

KOMBUCHA TEA

Meghan told lifestyle blog *Mind Body Green* that she's a fan of kombucha, a lightly effervescent, fermented tea. Made with tea, sugar, bacteria and yeast, the popular coffee alternative contains a whole colony of health-boosting bacteria and yeast.

WHY IT'S GOOD FOR YOU:

Kombucha is a great natural source of the gut-friendly probiotics that have been shown to help with digestion and may even help boost the immune system.

SUSHI

Meghan is a huge fan of the Japanese raw fish cuisine, describing "perfect sushi" as an essential part of her healthy diet in an interview with *EyeSwoon*.

WHY IT'S GOOD FOR YOU:

Tuna, salmon or other similar fish served raw as sushi are all a fantastic source of heart-healthy omega-3 fatty acids. Plus, fish is naturally low in calories and sugar.

WATERMELON

"I have always loved watermelon and relish any opportunity to eat it, whether plain or diced up with feta and mint and tossed with a little olive oil," Meghan revealed on US TV show *Today*. "It makes me think of summertime. I try to always have a container of watermelon sprinkled with cinnamon because it elevates the flavour just a notch, and makes it feel special."

WHY IT'S GOOD FOR YOU

Each bite of this juicy pink fruit contains significant levels of vitamins A, B6 and C, as well as lots of lycopene, antioxidants and amino acids. Lycopene has been linked with better heart health and helping to fight sun damage.

EGGS

Meghan often shared her love of egg-based meals on her former lifestyle blog *The Tig*, with a simple omelette with fresh herbs and cheese apparently an all-time favourite breakfast for her.

WHY IT'S GOOD FOR YOU

Eggs are a very good source of high-quality protein. Plus, the whites are rich sources of selenium, vitamins D, B6, B12 and minerals such as zinc, iron and copper.

QUINOA

Meghan has said before that quinoa is her go-to grain. "At the start of each week I generally cook a box of quinoa, and while it's simmering, I sauté onions, garlic and any veggies I have on hand in a separate pan," she told *Today*. "I always add crushed red pepper and chopped fresh herbs. Then I toss this veggie mixture into the finished quinoa and eat it as a side dish, poured on top of a kale salad, or as an easy snack."

WHY IT'S GOOD FOR YOU

Quinoa is gluten-free, high in protein and one of the few plant foods which contain all nine essential amino acids. It is also high in fibre, magnesium, B vitamins, iron, potassium, calcium, phosphorus, vitamin E and various beneficial antioxidants.

MEGHAN ON WINE

A good glass of wine, matched carefully to the dish you are eating, is one of life's finest pleasures for a true gourmet. And Meghan is no exception, speaking many times about her love for wine. As the former actress told Today *back in 2012, "At the end of a long day, there is nothing I enjoy more than a glass of wine."*

Indeed, it was Meghan's appreciation of wine that inspired the name of her lifestyle blog *The Tig*. As she explained once to *People*, "Tignanello is a full-bodied red wine that I tried about seven years ago. In wine circles, it's nicknamed 'Tig' and it was my first moment of 'getting it' – I finally understood what people meant by the body structure, finish, legs of wine. So *The Tig* is my nickname for me 'getting it'. Not just wine, but everything."

Created by Tuscan winery Marchesi Antinori in 1971, Tignanello is what's referred to as a "super-Tuscan" wine – a red wine made in Tuscany with non-indigenous grapes. It consists of a blend of three different varieties: 80 per cent Sangiovese, 15 per cent Cabernet Sauvignon and 5per cent Cabernet Franc. Tignanello is one of the earliest super Tuscan wines and one of the first Chianti reds not to use white grapes. This delicious wine went on to become a pricey but highly desirable label, wowing a huge number of fans, like Meghan, with its rich, full taste.

One thing to note, though, is the correct pronunciation. Although it is called "Tig" in America, this nickname is actually a little misleading. In Italian the "g" in Tignanello isn't pronounced at all – the name should be spoken as "teen-yah-neh-lo".

Beyond her favourite Tignanello, Meghan has noted that she enjoys a wide variety of wines. According to a story in food blog *Delish*, she is also a fan of Argentinian Malbecs, pinot noirs from Oregon, and, during the summer, "rosé all day".

As a native of California, with its many thousands of vineyards, Meghan has also described her delight in finding "off-the-beaten-path wineries" where "the exploration of finding a great wine is part of the fun". Writing for *Delish*, Meghan noted that the fun of hunting down a new label is "only trumped by that first sip of a pour that is made with such care that you can't help but want to thank the winemaker personally".

Meghan's keen interest in wine led many observers to speculate that she was behind the Californian wine chosen for the royal wedding. The Duke and Duchess of Sussex poured Domaine Eden Pinot Noir 2014 from Mount Eden Vineyards for their guests. Described as "raspberry scented and light" with a "little bit of spice", some nine cases were apparently ordered. "We're absolutely delighted that our wine was selected for the royal wedding," Mount Eden Vineyards co-owner and CEO Ellie Patterson told the *Food and Wine* website. "After all, the Santa Cruz Mountains American Viticultural Area is the birthplace of pinot noir in California, and our Domaine Eden Pinot Noir has balance and transparency that reflects the calibre of wines our region has to offer."

MEGHAN'S FOOD HOTSPOTS

The Duchess of Sussex has eaten in a huge number of restaurants around the world. Here are some of those thought to be her favourites.

BOCCA DI LUPO, LONDON, UK

Meghan fell in love with Italy's Amalfi Coast when she visited it – in particular the stunning hilltop town of Positano – so it's not surprising that she's been seen enjoying Italian food in London. One place she's been spotted dining is Soho haunt Bocca Di Lupo, a popular restaurant which enjoys a bustling vibe and lively atmosphere, and offers regional food and wine from right across Italy. The menu boasts artisan breads, sausages, salami, pickles and handmade pasta, with traditional homemade gelato to finish.

CHOTE CHITR, NEAR BANGKOK, THAILAND

"It's got about six tables. There's no Michelin star — it's not fancy," Meghan said of this small eatery some 20 minutes outside Thailand's capital. "I took one bite of pad thai and said, 'Oh my god, what have I been eating all my life? This is what pad thai's supposed to taste like?'" There's nothing pretentious about this food spot, which is one reason Meghan loves it. The focus is entirely on the food, served in the same traditional style it's been made for decades. Fans of the restaurant rave about a crispy noodle dish called mi krop (or mee krob), which has become an international favourite, but is very rarely made in the traditional Thai way on offer at Chote Chitr. Authentic mi krop includes garnishing the dish with the rind of a fragrant but hard-to-find local citrus fruit, called som saa. Another dish of note at Chote Chitr is the spicy banana flower salad, which is made using shredded banana flowers, toasted dried chilli peppers, fried shallots, coconut cream, shrimp, chicken and black sesame seeds.

DIAR IL-BNIET, DINGLI, MALTA

One of Meghan's all-time favourite getaways in Europe is Malta, and this restaurant is a hidden gem she wrote about on her blog. Not only did she love the restaurant's decor, particularly the typical Maltese floor tiles, she found the food delicious, too. Dorianne Kurtcu Mifsud, from Diar il-Bniet, reported that her famous guest had asked for a second serving of the fresh sheep cheeselettes – little cheese-filled pastries – and also enjoyed the rabbit and garlic spaghetti.

THE SANDS END, FULHAM, LONDON, UK

One of Prince Harry's oldest friends, Mark Dyer, owns this award-winning gastropub in Fulham, Southwest London, and Meghan and Harry enjoyed lunch there in 2016. The unpretentious pub serves up delicious Modern-British fare, along with a range of ales and an extensive wine list. Plus, dogs are allowed, which will have been a bonus for animal-lover Meghan.

3 DIVES RESTAURANT AND CLIFF BAR, NEGRIL, JAMAICA

Meghan loves spending time in the Negril area of this Caribbean island, which enjoys a dramatic coastline of caves and twisting inlets, along with some great places to eat. At 3 Dives – said to have the best jerk chicken in town – Meghan typically orders the grilled chicken and lobster, washed down with a Red Stripe beer. The Duchess has even described the "jerk sauce covering my face after a perfect meal" before apparently dancing to the house reggae band.

VIOLET BAKERY, HACKNEY, LONDON, UK

The owner of this cult bakery, Claire Ptak, was charged with making a delicious-sounding lemon and elderflower cake – complete with fresh spring flowers – for the royal wedding. Based in Hackney, Violets is known for making beautiful cupcakes with seasonally flavoured buttercreams, along with delectable cinnamon buns
and ginger and molasses cakes.

SUSHI PARK, LOS ANGELES, USA

When Californian girl Meghan described "perfect sushi" as an essential part of her healthy diet to blog *EyeSwoon*, she also added that Sushi Park on Sunset Boulevard is one of her all-time favourite restaurants. With a sign outside stating "No Trendy Sushi, No Salad, No Veggies, No California Roll, No Spicy Tuna Roll, No Teriyaki, No Tempura", the no-nonsense eatery clearly sets itself apart from your average sushi shop. But if you like your sushi simple and straightforward then inside you'll find melt-in-the-mouth delicacies such as blue crab hand roll and skipjack sashimi.

BLACKBIRD BAKING COMPANY, TORONTO, CANADA

While living in Toronto to film the TV series *Suits*, Meghan loved Pedestrian Sundays at Kensington Market – a foodie heaven, featuring stall after stall filled with delicacies to try. While shopping there, she was known to stop by the Blackbird Baking Company to pick up a loaf or two, according to its owner Simon Blackwell. Meghan even blogged about the Blackbird's Baldwin brown sourdough on her now-defunct lifestyle site *The Tig*. Made with Red Fife flour, Canada's oldest heritage wheat, this sourdough bread is thought to be gentler on the digestion because it's made using slowly fermented yeast.

MINETTA TAVERN, NEW YORK, USA

In an interview with *The Citiphile*, Meghan said she adored this restaurant in New York's Greenwich Village. "Sitting at the bar with a gorgeous glass of wine and a dozen oysters," she said of her favourite meal, "followed by the Black Label burger and french fries… and more wine!" The trendy spot is indeed particularly famous for the Black Label burger, which is known locally as "the greatest burger available in all of Manhattan". The $28 burger is comprised of prime, dry-aged beef cooked on a plancha with clarified butter, then nestled into a sesame-studded brioche bun designed specifically for it, topped simply with caramelized onions and served with pommes frites.

CHILTERN FIREHOUSE, LONDON, UK

This exclusive restaurant has been the place to be seen at in London since it opened in 2013. Meghan has been snapped going to this celebrity hangout several times. She is said to be a fan of their Negroni cocktails – made of equal parts gin, vermouth and Campari. The creative British cuisine from chef Nuno Mendes is also a highlight for those lucky enough to get a table, with dishes on the menu such as salmon and caviar on cod skins and lobster omelette.

HO

ME

Meghan

HOME

MEGHAN'S "MAKE YOUR HOUSE A HOME" TIPS

As someone who travels a great deal, Meghan has spoken at length about how important a comfortable home is to her – a sanctuary to return to after trips away. After all, as she once told her 1.6 million Instagram followers, "There's no place like home."

Indeed, Meghan's archive of Instagram posts reveals her to be an aspiring interior designer, with a real flair for creating a stylish abode. Before becoming engaged to Prince Harry, Meghan posted many photos of her beautiful apartment in Toronto, giving her followers a huge insight into the kind of decor, furniture and colours that the actress favoured. Her former home, which was beautifully appointed with a well-balanced blend of cozy and cool, serves as clear guide to her home-styling rules.

BRING IN THE SUNSHINE – ALL YEAR ROUND

The laidback LA style aesthetic – so evident in Meghan's dress sense – was also apparent in her Toronto home, with plenty of natural sunlight allowed to flow into rooms. Indeed, the former actress even credits her sunny decor with helping her survive, "seven Canadian winters". And although royal etiquette means we're unlikely to ever see inside her new Kensington Palace apartment, it's likely that the Duchess will retain her love of natural light, not least to help brighten up the drearier English days.

KEEP YOUR COLOUR PALETTE SIMPLE

It's evident Meghan prefers bright, neutral colours, with every room in her former Toronto apartment decorated in crisp and clean shades of beige, cream and white. Her dining table was also a beautiful white marble. And despite having two dogs, with all that potential for shedding fur and muddy paws, the actress bravely opted for a white couch. Pale, flowing window drapes and white linens on her beds completed the light-as-air look and created a dreamy yet sophisticated vibe.

ADD A POP OF COLOUR WITH ACCESSORIES

Rather than choose to paint her walls in bright shades, the former actress used vibrant accessories to add a splash of colour to her rooms and prevent the overall look becoming too sterile or boring. Stacks of books, rows of designer shoes, vases of fresh flowers and carefully curated touches, such as a red striped hallway rug, all added welcome dashes to the neutral palette.

BLEND AFFORDABLE BASICS WITH LUXURY ONE-OFFS

Just as she does with her fashion outfits, Meghan expertly mixed high- and low-price items throughout her apartment. Some pictures show a red striped IKEA rug with one of her dogs curled up on it, right underneath an expensive original painting. This is a sign of someone who knows what she likes and is confident to search for items that she loves anywhere and everywhere. This is also a classic interior designer trick – choosing lower price-point items for the basics which nobody will realize are budget buys, and saving your cash to splash out on a few show-stopping items that really catch the eye and repay the investment.

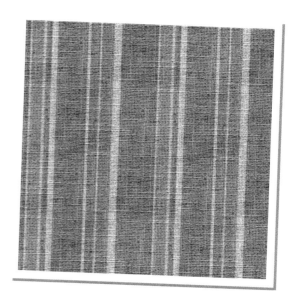

MIX UP YOUR STYLES

Meghan's Toronto pad had a very modern, eclectic feel. This perfectly imperfect mix of styles is also a direct reflection of her personal clothing style. The pretty home included Scandinavian-style modern furniture, such as the pale dining table, next to items with a more Boho feel, such as the Moroccan Beni Ourain wool rug which sat under it. In her bedroom Meghan chose an oversized, black wrought-iron birdcage design for the bed, which lends a more industrial edge to the space. The overall result is an authentic, lived-in look which remains incredibly stylish.

" *THIS PERFECTLY IMPERFECT MIX OF STYLES IS ALSO A DIRECT REFLECTION OF HER PERSONAL CLOTHING STYLE.* "

PLACE COMFORT OVER FUSS

Like any true homebody Meghan has talked in the past about how she loves a good "staycation". In one post to her lifestyle blog *The Tig* she encouraged her followers to make the most of their relaxing days at home by turning off technology and doing a "mental detox". As befits a home meant for extended relaxation, the Toronto flat was filled with soft, comfort-inducing touches, including slouchy-looking chairs and sofas, soft cushions and tactile cashmere and sheepskin throws.

A PLACE FOR EVERYTHING

Like any self-respecting fashion icon Meghan has an extensive collection of shoes that only continues to expand to match the many new outfits her royal role demands. To house this impressive collection in her Toronto flat, she had an entire shelving unit dedicated to displaying her favourites, including heels from the likes of Christian Louboutin, Miu Miu and Sarah Flint. In fact, so much does Meghan love displaying her favourite footwear, she once spent an entire sick day at home rearranging them – sharing the impressive results on Instagram. The revealing shot highlighted Meghan's neat-freak credentials and also a more colourful side, as her shoe ensemble included pairs that were bold red, fuchsia and leopard print.

EXPRESS YOURSELF WITH ART

A key way to personalize your home and bring it to life is by filling it with pictures that you love and that mean something special to you. Meghan appreciates fine art and has a good eye for pieces, showcasing a print by photographer Gray Malin of a bird's-eye view of a beach on the wall of her former living area. Above the bed in the guest room hung a watercolour of a figure by trendy New York based artist and illustrator Inslee Fariss.

COLOUR CODE YOUR BOOKS

Clearly someone who likes everything in order, Meghan arranged the books in her old apartment in colour blocks and showed the results off on Instagram. This rainbow patterning effect has been very much in vogue in recent years and helps create both visual interest and order to bookshelves, which can otherwise appear dull or a bit haphazard. Her micro-organization skills appear to have impressed her online fans, with one noting excitedly, "Colour coded books!"

CREATE A GARDEN HAVEN

As someone who loves nature and the great outdoors, Meghan would never leave a garden area neglected. In Toronto she grew her own hydrangeas in the garden, which she would often cut and place in jam jars to decorate the apartment. She also made great use of the small outside space with a seating area plus wooden decking, a large BBQ and a black metal love seat with monochrome striped cushions. Perfect for entertaining.

THOSE FINISHING TOUCHES

Meghan knows instinctively that, when it comes to covetable interiors, finding statement pieces and dotting them artfully around helps to warm up a space and add further interest. Be it gorgeous fresh flowers, scented candles and room diffusers to add a romantic touch, or intriguing art and interesting books to show a more thoughtful side, Meghan has a skill for adding those little details that make all the difference. Here are some of her all-time favourites ...

HOTEL-STYLE BED LINEN

For Meghan it must be high thread-count, white bed linen that looks "perfectly crisp and ironed". Sheets like this, she says, will make any home instantly feel like a "boutique hotel".

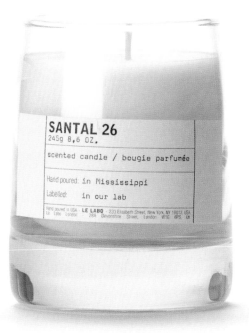

PRETTY PHOTO FRAMES

Meghan's old place showcased plenty of metallic and patterned photo frames. We all have favourite photographs, but placing them in gorgeous frames will help make any place feel like home straight away.

SCENTED CANDLES

Photos of Meghan's previous home show that, like many of us, she loves a luxury scented candle to help create a relaxed atmosphere. Diptyque's Figuier Candle was once spotted on the side table of her Toronto flat. This cult Parisian candle maker is famed for its gorgeous scents and stylish packaging. Figuier is a delectable blend of fresh wood, green notes and crushed fig leaves. Another candle once photographed in her home is the Santal 26 Classic Candle, from trendy New York brand Le Labo, which has "gentle, smokey and leathery tones".

STYLISH MIRRORS

In one old photograph of Meghan's former home, a beautiful shabby-chic, vintage mirror rested on the wall behind her white marble dining table. A favourite trick of interior designers, clever placement of a mirror helps create the illusion of extra space in smaller rooms and can also reflect light from a window to brighten an otherwise dark area.

FLOWER POWER

Meghan adores displaying fresh flowers in her home, especially pink peonies, an all-time favourite she's declared make her "so endlessly happy". But rather than waiting to be bought flowers by others, the Duchess revealed in the past that she regularly cuts them from her own garden or treats herself to shop-bought bouquets – encouraging others to follow suit and "do something sweet for yourself today too".

LUXURY THROWS

Understanding the power of a pretty, soft throw, Meghan had cosy blankets all over her old apartment. In Toronto this included soft cashmere throws on the beds and furry sheepskins over the backs of wicker chairs. Not only do tactile throws like this add comfort, they also help create an interesting combination of textures in a room. One old Instagram picture featured a grey striped throw from the luxury Canadian textiles brand Pamuk & Co, which specializes in traditional Turkish "towels" made from high-quality cotton that are also useful as shawls, yoga mats and picnic blankets.

COFFEE TABLE BOOKS

A huge fan of proper "reading" books, Meghan also enjoys having a
selection of style and photography books to flick through on the coffee
table or sideboard. Titles spotted on her coffee tables in the past have
included French *Vogue* editor Carine Roitfeld's style autobiography and
a book of Linda McCartney's most iconic photographs. These books are
often artfully arranged around the house, becoming design features in their
own right by being placed underneath jugs of flowers or other ornaments.

TRA

VEL

Meghan

TRAVEL

MEGHAN'S PASSPORT STAMPS: 16 PLACES THE DUCHESS ADORES AND WHY SHE LOVES THEM

Long before she was touring the Commonwealth with husband Prince Harry, Meghan was already a frequent flyer and wrote regularly about her travels on her now-closed lifestyle blog The Tig.

A glance through these old posts proves that Meghan has always been a bona fide jetsetter who adores travelling and has visited dozens of countries all over the world, with passport stamps from Istanbul, Turkey, Cartagena, Colombia and Melbourne, Australia, to name but a few.

Nor is the California gal afraid of some serious longhaul – after all, during her time shooting *Suits*, the star regularly made the journey from her working home in Toronto to her native Los Angeles and back again. She also squeezed in girls' trips to Italy and Spain, before numerous visits to London to see Prince Harry.

And now Meghan's new formal role as the Duchess of Sussex will require even more travel, from fleeting official engagements to longer royal tours, such as the one she and Harry made of Tonga, Fiji, New Zealand and Australia in October 2018.

But for Meghan following the tourist crowds has never been what she looks for in a trip. "I always want off-the-beaten path," she told *Marie Claire* in 2013, citing what she called "Anthony Bourdain-inspired travel" after the late globe-trotting chef. From actress to duchess, Meghan has been hot-footing it around the world for years. Here are some of her favourite trips and travel highlights.

> " *TRAVELING GIVES YOU SOME PERSPECTIVE OF WHAT THE REST OF THE WORLD IS LIKE. I THINK THAT HAVING THE COURAGE TO STEP OUT OF THE NORM IS THE MOST IMPORTANT THING.* "
>
> *INTERVIEW WITH* THE CHICAGO TRIBUNE, *2013*

NEGRIL, JAMAICA

Meghan wrote on *The Tig* of a life-changing trip to Jamaica with her mother as a 10-year-old. Meghan's subsequent trips to Negril, Jamaica, were so incredible that she almost didn't write about it so she could keep the "specific sliver of paradise" to herself. But she did eventually describe this Jamaican idyll, recommending morning beach yoga, cliff jumping, diving for sea urchins, climbing ackee trees with the locals and eating jerk salmon sandwiches as things not to miss.

Meghan – who wed first husband Trevor Engelson at Ocho Rios's Jamaica Inn in 2011 continues to hold a candle for Negril today. Her chosen base is often the Rockhouse Hotel, a boutique hotel hewn from volcanic rock, where the thatched beach villas have outdoor showers. She also returned to Jamaica in March 2018 to accompany Prince Harry to the wedding of his friend, Tom Inskip, in Montego Bay, some 50 miles further north from Negril.

This time the couple reportedly checked into one of the luxury villas (starting from about $2,000 a night) at the super-exclusive Round Hill Hotel and Villas. The 50-year-old hotel is decorated in the traditional Jamaican colonial style by Ralph Lauren, giving it a luxurious but understated and discrete feel, befitting royalty.

POSITANO, ITALY

Meghan spent a month in Italy in August 2016 with her good friend and stylist Jessica Mulroney, while taking a break from filming *Suits*. Inspired by reading Elizabeth Gilbert's famous memoir about her time in Italy, *Eat Pray Love*, Meghan said she planned to, "eat everything, pray (and meditate) often, and simply love my life, every ounce of it". This fabulous trip proved to be one of her last jaunts as a single girl before meeting Prince Harry.

Meghan's primary destination was the stunning Amalfi Coast, where she opted to stay at the family-run cliffside hotel Le Sirenuse in the picturesque town of Positano. She posted pictures of her stay in Italy, enjoying local pizzas, drinks at sunset with her friend and walking around the local sights in her trainers. One picture showed the two women relaxing on sun loungers with cocktails in hand, which Mulroney captioned, "Girls trip has officially begun with @ meghanmarkle (which means don't bother me unless you have to)".

NEW YORK

Although a born and bred Californian, Meghan adores the bustle and very different vibe of New York, with the Lower East Side one of her favourite neighbourhoods. Meghan has been known to clink glasses at The Bowery Hotel, which she has praised for its "cosy charm and the who's who nightlife scene".

Often when she's in town these days, Meghan drops off her bags at the chic Greenwich Village hotel, The Marlton (below). She has talked before about how much she loves the hotel's central location and how it offers everything from comforting drinks by the lobby fire to charming bedrooms and a fabulously smart in-house restaurant. She particularly recommended the penthouse with its old-style herringbone floor and claw-footed roll-top bath.

Outside Manhattan, Brooklyn is another favourite Meghan haunt and apparently the most fun when your goal is eating and drinking!

BOTSWANA, SOUTHERN AFRICA

It was in this breathtaking country, with its spectacular wildlife, dramatic rivers and Kalahari Desert sands, that Prince Harry and Meghan enjoyed their first official date in August 2016. Somewhat unusually, that took the form of a five-day holiday. "I managed to persuade her to come and join me in Botswana, and we camped out with each other under the stars," the Prince revealed during the couple's engagement interview.

The new couple stayed at Meno a Kwena tented camp, a hideaway sandwiched between the Okavango Delta and Central Kalahari Game Reserve. The Prince is such a fixture here – interestingly, Harry also took his ex, Chelsy Davy, to the reserve in 2007 – that the staff call him by his first name. The entire camp is stunning, ideally situated to see animals on safari and enjoy scenic flights over the local salt flats. Guests can even watch elephants bathing in waterholes from the comfort of their luxury tent, as they take their own bath in a rose-petal topped tub.

ISTANBUL, TURKEY

The former capital of Turkey, the beautiful and historic city of Istanbul, has been on Meghan's travel itinerary several times. It was during one stay here that she met French fashion designer Roland Mouret in a hotel lift and the pair became good friends – with Meghan wearing many of his celebrated dresses since. "This man in a bathrobe said, 'I'd love to dress you'," Meghan later revealed of that first encounter. "I thought, 'Whaaat?' Then he told me who he was and we've been friends ever since." Following one whirlwind 48-hour visit, Meghan recommended to her blog followers the Grand Bazaar (right) for authentic Turkish rugs, Kiya restaurant for fresh seafood, and for a traditional Turkish bath experience either the Cemberlitas Hamami or the Kilic Ali Pasa Hamam.

TROMSØ, NORWAY

In January 2018, Meghan and Harry holidayed together in Tromsø, the Norwegian city that boasts the world's most annual sightings of the aurora borealis. This spectacular light show, commonly known as the Northern Lights, brings millions of tourists to the area each year in the hope of glimpsing it. Tromsø itself is gateway to the Scandinavian tundra, and is a picture postcard blend of gingerbread-shaped houses, fancy art galleries and hot chocolate bars – all surrounded by the area's famous snow-covered fjords. The town is also an extremely popular base for many typical Arctic activities. The couple – who stayed in an isolated, no-frills lodge – are said to have enjoyed whale watching and a trip to Prestvannet (above), a frozen lake which acts as an enormous mirror to the green-glowing aerial acrobatics of the aurora borealis.

MADRID, SPAIN

In 2002, while taking her degree in International Studies at Northwestern University, Meghan had the opportunity to travel and study with IES Abroad (The Institute for the International Education of Students) in Madrid. This gave her the chance to practise her Spanish and engage in the culture, cuisine and history of Spain's vibrant capital city. These fond memories were no doubt foremost in her mind when she visited Madrid again with two friends, Markus Anderson and Misha Nonoo, in 2016. While there, she toured the Museo Prado – Spain's world renowned art museum – ate plenty of tapas and even danced in the streets.

VANCOUVER, CANADA

Although Meghan was born and raised in Los Angeles, Canada became her second home for the eight years she shot TV series *Suits* there. And, of course, Prince Harry spent a lot of time visiting her there during the early days of their courtship. Although she was based in Toronto for filming, the actress also spent a fair amount of time on the country's west coast, with Vancouver a favourite haunt. "Dear Vancouver, I really, really love you," she captioned one Instagram post, "so many good memories in this city."

Squamish, a town north of Vancouver – known as "the outdoor recreation capital of Canada", thanks to its epic climbing rocks – also found its way into her heart during filming there, with Meghan labelling it a place "so pretty it hurts".

OAXACA, MEXICO

Meghan has visited Mexico regularly since childhood, even if the travel came with some eye-opening experiences. "Taking trips to Oaxaca, Mexico, I saw children play in the dirt roads, peddling chiclets (chewing gum) for a few extra pesos to bring home," Meghan wrote on *The Tig* of these first childhood trips. "My mother raised me to be a global citizen, with eyes open to sometimes harsh realities."

But Mexico also stands out for many other reasons. The actress has said that one of her most vivid childhood memories is travelling to Oaxaca for the Day of the Dead festival, where the nine-year old Meghan apparently ate a lot of "moles" – a traditional hot dish made from chocolate and chilli. "The culture, food, people and varied landscapes make Mexico a favoured destination of mine year after year," Meghan says now.

Another special spot she has talked about visiting and enjoying is Sayulita, a hippy fishing village and surfing hub on Mexico's Pacific coast. This offbeat destination is renowned for its seafood tacos, beautiful beaches and what Meghan calls its "boho-chic sensibility".

Meghan's father is also based in Mexico and she has previously spent time relaxing in the resort town of Tulum in Baja California, in the country's north. This low-key beach destination is a pretty mix of blue volcanoes, humpback whales and Asian-influenced cuisine. Meghan particularly loved having a traditional Mayan clay beauty treatment there, along with practicing beach yoga and touring the local ruins of Chichén Itzá (right), the country's largest remains of an ancient Mayan city.

BUDAPEST, HUNGARY

Megan filmed part of a movie she starred in, called *Anti-Social*, in Budapest in 2015. And in her blog post about the city she described the Hungarian capital as one of the most "visually stunning" places she's ever visited. She also reminisced about morning runs along the Danube and eating pastries at one of the oldest cafés in Budapest, Ruszwurm.

DUBLIN, IRELAND

On Meghan and Harry's royal visit to Ireland, Meghan told a fan that Dublin is her favourite city. This may be because the former actress has some confirmed Irish roots, details of which she was presented with when she visited EPIC, The Irish Emigration Museum in Dublin. Genealogists found links to a Mary McCague of Ballinasloe, who was born in 1829 and went on to marry a British Army soldier, Thomas Bird, who was stationed in Ireland at the time.

During their official stay Meghan and Harry had lunch at Delahunt, a contemporary Irish restaurant and bar situated in an historic Victorian building on Dublin's Camden Street, and learned more about Irish history at the Famine Memorial and the Book of Kells. These statues commemorate the Great Famine of the mid-nineteenth century, during which a million people died and a million more emigrated from Ireland, causing the island's population to fall by some 25 per cent.

VALLETTA, MALTA

The Duchess of Sussex also has personal connections with the Mediterranean island of Malta, as her great-great-grandmother Mary was born there in 1862. She called her visit there in 2015 "the most breathtaking trip in the most remarkable place." Meghan particularly rated the eight-suite Casa Ellul in Valletta (above) as her "favourite property" for its "Calvin Klein meets *Game of Thrones*" interiors. And she was also enthralled by St John's Co-Cathedral, a spectacular Baroque church built in 1573, in which the only signed painting by Italian master Caravaggio hangs.

When it came to Maltese cuisine Meghan sampled the rabbit spaghetti at Diar il-Bniet, a restaurant-cum-larder in Dingli, and dined at Meridiana, a winery owned by the Antinori family. She also recommended heading to Gozo – a tiny island only accessible by boat from Malta to experience "seafood heaven".

Of her time on the island Meghan told Maltese website *LittleRock*, "I've been fortunate to travel all over the world and I love a different cultural experience wherever you go, but to come somewhere where you so quickly settle in to feeling welcomed is really special; it's this Maltese hospitality that is really special to the place."

HYDRA, GREECE

Meghan selected this Greek destination (right) for a low-key hen weekend for her close friend from university, the author Lindsay Roth. Hydra is a secluded island two hours by boat from Athens. Bikes and donkeys are the only ways to travel around it and there's not much to do, which makes it an ideal place to decompress. As Meghan wrote on her website, "There is something wholly cathartic about being able to turn it all off – to sunbathe with no one watching, swim in the briny Mediterranean Sea, eat copious amounts of Greek salads and fried red mullets, and toast to the day."

She also recommended taking a stroll around the town centre or trying the small tavernas for local tzatziki and Ouzo. After lunch, Meghan's routine was just as simple, "Take a swim, then a nap, hike back to your hotel or apartment ... rinse and repeat."

HAFNARFJORDUR, ICELAND

The somewhat chilly Icelandic climate might make it a bit cooler than your average holiday destination, but its breathtaking beauty wins over many visitors – Meghan included. After spending New Year 2016 in Iceland, the former actress wrote on her Instagram, "Let's do this again sometime soon. You're so pretty, and really nice too. Just my type." While in Iceland she visited Hafnarfjordur (below), south of Reykjavik, known as "the town of elves". It is said to be home to one of the country's largest settlements of "hidden folk", with many Icelanders still believing in this traditional folklore today.

MILAN, ITALY

An established lover of all things Italian, Meghan described the highlight of her trip to Milan, in a personal guide on her blog, as "sheets of hand-torn pasta woven through luscious bolognese". She also recommended the Medieval winding streets of the Brera district, home to many galleries for art fans, and Il Montalcino, a Tuscan-themed restaurant for dinner. Also on this early trip to Italy Meghan recalled, "Flirting with boys in Venice, when my best friend and I backpacked through the country for Spring Break ... the perfection of a scoop of Nutella gelato dripping down your chin."

LONDON, UK

London is no longer a holiday spot for Meghan, with the Duke and Duchess of Sussex now residing permanently in their Kensington Palace apartment. But the truth is, Britain's capital city has long held a special place in Meghan's heart. As far back as 2013, when interviewed on the red carpet for the Global Gift Gala in London, she joked "It is very cold, but the people are so warm. As cheesy as that sounds, I was joking today that I've never been called 'love' or 'darling' more in my life, so it makes me want to stick around for a while." And stick around she did, to enjoy all that one of the world's most cosmopolitan cities has to offer – be that catching a musical in the West End, as she did when she watched hit show *Hamilton* in August 2018 (below), or hanging out at exclusive members' club Soho House, allegedly where she first met Prince Harry.

Meghan has also been spotted leaving famed skin expert Sarah Chapman's Sloane Square beauty clinic after a treatment, and picking up bunches of flowers at Kensington Flower Corner. This long-running flower stall on the corner of Kensington High Street – just around the corner from the royal couple's palatial home – is something of an institution for locals and must thrill Meghan, who has often talked of her love of flowers around the house.

MEGHAN'S SMART PACKING TRICKS

Of course, with all these Air Miles under her belt, the Duchess has learnt some great travel tricks – many of which she shared on her former lifestyle blog, The Tig. *Here are some of the best.*

STOW A SNUGGLY SCARF

In the past the stylish Royal has admitted that there's one item she simply can't hit the road without. "I never travel without a scarf or thin cashmere blanket that feels like a hug," she wrote on her blog. "Throw it in your purse or backpack, and no matter how far you travel, you will always feel comforted, both on and off the plane. This has become invaluable to me when catching some Zzzzzs on a flight, or feeling swaddled in a hotel room," she explained.

FRESHEN UP YOUR PACKING

Meghan shared a genius hack for ensuring that your clothes stay fresh – even after being stashed in a suitcase – during a collaboration with online beauty store Birchbox. She suggests layering tumble dryer sheets – those thin bits of paper impregnated with fabric freshener that you stick in the tumble dryer – between your shirts, skirts and dresses when you pack. "Your clothes will smell fresh when you arrive – and especially when you return home," she enthused.

EAT TO BEAT JET LAG

Meghan has long followed some travel advice passed on by her good friend the designer Misha Nonoo, who once explained that if you adjust your eating to the time schedule of the country where you've landed, you won't feel jet lagged. "By simply eating a meal at the time the locals are when you land, you trick your brain a bit and stay much more on track, and much less cranky," Meghan wrote on *The Tig*.

TAKE SOME TEA TREE OIL

Meghan once told *Allure*, "The one thing that I cannot live without when I'm travelling is a small container of tea tree oil. It's not the most glamorous thing, but if you get a cut, a mosquito bite, a small breakout, no matter what it is, it's my little cure-all." Tea tree oil is an essential oil that acts as an antiseptic, meaning it helps keep germs at bay and can quickly soothe and disinfect a small wound or bug bite.

BEAT MID-AIR BUGS

Planes are a travelling time bomb of germs, thanks to them being trapped for hours in a cabin with recycled air. This makes planes one of the worst places for picking up colds and flu. However, Meghan has a handy trick for trying to minimize the spread of bugs. "I'm no germaphobe, but when I get to my plane seat I always use some quick hand wipes or a travel sanitizer spray to wipe it all down," she explained. "That includes the little TV, the service tray, and all the buttons around your seat."

CHA

RITY

Meghan

CHARITY

MEGHAN'S MISSION: THE CAUSES DEAR TO THE DUCHESS'S HEART

No portrait of Meghan can be complete without making reference to the political and charitable ideals that have long played a significant role in her life. Since first volunteering aged just 13 at a soup kitchen on Skid Row, an infamously poor area of Los Angeles, Meghan has worked tirelessly to help those less fortunate than herself. She later leveraged her fame as an actress to create awareness for charitable organizations – and it's clear that she will use the even greater platform afforded her as a member of the Royal Family to continue to advocate for those without a voice.

In fact, Meghan has been vocal on this point, having used her engagement announcement to Prince Harry as an opportunity to reveal that she was leaving acting behind to focus solely on philanthropy. So, to complete our picture of Meghan, in this chapter we take a closer look at the key charities she has worked with and why they are so important to her.

ONE YOUNG WORLD

This youth charity's stated mission is to "gather young leaders from around the world, help them make lasting connections and create positive change". Meghan was a counsellor at One Young World Summits in Dublin, Ireland, in 2014 and Ottawa, Canada, in 2016 (right). At this summit she delivered a talk alongside Canadian president Justin Trudeau and famously accused the creator of her own show, *Suits*, of gender inequality for requiring her character to do so many semi-naked scenes on the show.

WORLD VISION

Meghan became a World Vision global ambassador after travelling to Rwanda with the charity in February 2016 (opposite). She saw first-hand the impact that clean water has on the lives of children and communities in the developing world, visiting school students who enjoyed access to a clean water pipeline as a result of World Vision's work. Meghan's particular focus with World Vision was on women's health and education issues in the developing world. And although she has now left her official role there, it's expected that she will continue advocating for these issues globally in her capacity as the Duchess of Sussex.

MAP OF RWANDA
UGANDA
D.R-CONGO
NYAGATARE
MUSANZE
BURERA
RUBAVU
GAKENKE
GICUMBI
GATSIBO
RURINDO
KAYONZA
RUTSIRO
MUHANGA
GASABO
KICUKIRO
RWAMAGANA
KIREHE

MYNA MAHILA FOUNDATION

As part of her work with World Vision, Meghan travelled to India and worked alongside this entrepreneurial Indian foundation that helps women to manufacture sanitary pads to sell in their communities. This work not only provides these products to girls, but also fosters open communication about women's menstruation. Meghan later wrote an article for *TIME* magazine about her experience, called "How Periods Affect Potential". She had seen first-hand how a lack of access to tampons and pads can hinder a woman's potential. "I traveled to Delhi and Mumbai to meet girls and women directly impacted by the stigmatization of menstrual health and to learn how it hinders girls' education," she wrote. "One hundred and thirteen million adolescent girls between the ages of 12–14 in India alone are at risk of dropping out of school because of the stigma surrounding menstrual health." This commitment to enabling a more open discussion of this, and other women's topics seen as taboo, is a key part of Meghan's larger advocacy for women's issues in the developing world.

UN WOMEN

For several years leading up to her marriage Meghan was an advocate for UN Women. In 2015 she narrated a public service announcement for the organization and also gave her now-famous speech before UN Secretary General Ban Ki-moon and the UN Forum for International Women's Day, where she declared, "I am proud to be a woman and a feminist." In another show of her staunch feminist principles, in March 2018, Meghan and Harry attended an event to celebrate and encourage women and girls in STEM in Birmingham, UK (below).

MEGHAN AND HARRY'S WEDDING CHARITIES

To mark the occasion of their marriage on 19 May 2018, the Duke and Duchess of Sussex asked guests and well-wishers to donate to a chosen charity rather than buying them a gift.

As the official spokesperson for Kensington Palace said before the wedding, "Prince Harry and Ms Meghan Markle are incredibly grateful for the goodwill shown to them since the announcement of their engagement and are keen that as many people as possible benefit from this generosity of spirit."

Together the couple chose seven charities reflecting a range of causes from ocean conservation to the Armed Forces. They also showed a determination to continue Princess Diana's work in support of people with HIV by choosing a children's charity in the same area. As the official statement said of the eclectic mix of good causes, "'Prince Harry and Ms Markle do not have any formal relationships with the charities chosen. The couple have chosen charities which represent a range of issues that they are passionate about. Many of these are small charities, and the couple are pleased to be able to amplify and shine a light on their work."

Here are the seven charities they chose ...

CHIVA (CHILDREN'S HIV ASSOCIATION)

CHIVA (below) supports children growing up with HIV across the UK and Ireland, ensuring they achieve their greatest potential. Upon learning of the happy couple's decision Dr Amanda Williams, chair of CHIVA, said, "We are delighted and honoured that Prince Harry and Ms Meghan Markle have chosen to recognise our work supporting the health and wellbeing of children and young people living with HIV in the UK and Ireland. We are grateful for the opportunity to raise awareness of the complex issues for young people growing up with HIV. We are a very small charity and through our work we support over 1,000 young people living with HIV. All donations will make a significant difference to our programmes of work and lead to direct improvements in the lives of these young people."

CRISIS

The national charity for homeless people, Crisis directly helps individuals to move out of homelessness, working side by side with thousands of people each year to assist them in rebuilding their lives. Chief executive Jon Sparkes said, "We are hugely grateful that Prince Harry and Ms Markle are asking the public to support Crisis as they celebrate their wedding. Homelessness is one of the most urgent issues of our time, but at Crisis we know what it takes to end it. Donations will help us to support more people to leave homelessness behind through our housing, employment, education and advice services across the country, and to campaign for the changes needed to solve the homelessness crisis once and for all."

MYNA MAHILA FOUNDATION

This initiative, which Megan first discovered on her 2016 trip to India with World Vision, empowers women in Mumbai's urban slums. It provides them with a trusted network which supports them professionally and personally, to help them grow as individuals and businesswomen. It offers women from these communities stable employment close to their homes, and breaks taboos around menstrual hygiene by offering access to low-cost sanitary pads and accurate information at their doorstep.

Suhani Jalota, who founded Myna Mahila in 2015, said, "Myna Mahila Foundation is delighted to be a part of this special occasion for Ms Meghan Markle and Prince Harry. This support will enable us to expand our reach into more urban slums in Mumbai, empowering local women through access to menstrual hygiene products and employment opportunities."

STREETGAMES

Using participation sport to change lives across the UK, StreetGames helps people and communities become healthier, safer and more successful. StreetGames sees sport as a perfect way to engage and empower young people, kick-starting a cycle of positive change that then resonates in the communities they live in. Jane Ashworth OBE, CEO of StreetGames said, "All of us at StreetGames are absolutely thrilled to have been personally chosen by Prince Harry and Ms Markle. It's a great honour to have our work using sport to change lives and communities recognised in this way."

ABOVE: Prince Harry plays with children at a 'Fit and Fed' summer holiday activity session, an initiative run by the StreetGames charity in London in July 2017.

SCOTTY'S LITTLE SOLDIERS

A charity which supports children who have lost a parent while serving in the British Armed Forces. The charity was set up by war widow Nikki Scott in memory of her late husband and father to her two children, Corporal Lee Scott, after he was killed in Afghanistan in 2009. Scotty's now provides assistance to hundreds of bereaved Forces children around the UK, including holidays, group events and bereavement counselling.

Founder Nikki Scott said, "We are absolutely overwhelmed to have been personally selected by Prince Harry and Meghan Markle as one of their chosen charities to benefit from donations marking the royal

wedding. For all our members Scotty's Little Soldiers offers a vital support network for children, who at such a young age, have already gone through so much. Simply having the opportunity to spend time with other children who have gone through something similar, or receiving a gift on the anniversary of their parent's death, can help reassure them that they are not alone."

ABOVE: When at Hampton Court Flower Show in 2015, Camilla Duchess of Cornwall spent some time looking at the Scotty's Little Soldiers' sponsored garden.

SURFERS AGAINST SEWAGE

This national marine conservation and campaigning charity works to inspire, unite and empower communities to take action to protect oceans, beaches, waves and wildlife. Chief executive Hugo Tagholm said, "Surfers Against Sewage is thrilled to be one of the charities chosen to benefit from donations marking the wedding of Prince Harry and Ms Meghan Markle. Our work as a national marine conservation charity empowers tens of thousands of volunteers annually to protect beaches for everyone. We are currently focused on tackling plastic pollution and this support will help us move towards our vision of plastic-free coastlines."

BELOW: A keen environmentalist, Prince Charles is also an avid supporter of the charity Surfers Against Sewage. Here he can be seen visiting the charity's headquarters in St Agnes, Cornwall, in July 2015.

THE WILDERNESS FOUNDATION UK

This charity, promoting the benefits and enjoyment of wild nature and bringing science to life in the great outdoors, helps build the resilience of vulnerable teenagers and also introduces rural employment to urban youth. CEO Jo Roberts said, "We are deeply touched and honoured that Prince Harry and Ms Markle have chosen to support The Wilderness Foundation and its beneficiaries. As the world's population grows exponentially the planet's remaining wild places and resources are coming under increasing threat. It has never been more important for us as humans to protect the planet that gives us life. Whilst teaching conservation values, we in turn use the positive power of nature to support and recharge the lives of challenged and vulnerable young people and adults."

ABOVE: Prince Harry tries nettle tea with Felstead Prep School year 7 pupils as he visits The Chatham Green Project, an initiative run by the Wilderness Foundation in Essex, 2017 .

OF ROYAL CONCERN:
MEGHAN'S NEW CHARITY WORK AS DUCHESS

Although Meghan's role as Duchess of Sussex has meant ending her affiliation with the charities she worked with before becoming a Royal, it's already clear that her work in this area will only increase in the future. Indeed, in April 2018, the official Windsor website announced that following the royal wedding on 19 May, Meghan "will perform Royal duties in support of the Queen through engagements at home and overseas, alongside a growing portfolio of charitable work and patronages".

While that portfolio is very much in the early stages, the best guide to the kind of causes the Duchess will embrace in the future remains the areas close to her heart before her marriage to Harry. For instance, given Meghan's history working with World Vision, One Young World and UN Women before she met Prince Harry, Royal observers have predicted her chosen charities will target poverty, youth issues and gender equality.

Speaking to *Express.co.uk* before the wedding, Royal commentator Richard Fitzwilliams said: "I expect Meghan to hit the ground running in areas such as female empowerment, especially as her commitment to feminism is mentioned on the Palace website". Mr Fitzwilliams continued, "Expect her to choose fewer causes than some of the other royals but to be more hands-on and to have an incredible global reach as a senior member of the Royal Family. As someone who identifies as bi-racial, she is ideally placed to champion diversity, which she undoubtedly will."

It's also already apparent that Meghan will embrace some of the charities close to Prince Harry's heart, which have centred on working with mental health issues and members of the Armed Forces and their families. Here, we review what Meghan's early acts and appearances as a Royal signal for her future portfolio of patronages and charities.

THE ROYAL FOUNDATION

The first role put in place for Meghan was working alongside Harry and the Duke and Duchess of Cambridge. Four months before her wedding, Buckingham Palace announced that the future Duchess of Sussex would become a patron of The Royal Foundation, an organization Princes Harry and William founded in 2011 to pursue philanthropic interests, with a specific focus on mental health issues. Joining Kate as well as Harry and William, Meghan became the Foundation's fourth patron – officially changing the title to the more evenly balanced The Royal Foundation of the Duke and Duchess of Cambridge and the Duke and Duchess of Sussex.

The Foundation is behind programmes personally important to the younger Royals, such as the Heads Together mental health campaign, and also works in many areas including the Armed Forces, young people and conservation. Meghan's first public engagement for the Foundation was speaking at their annual forum in February 2018, when she announced that she was indeed ready to "hit the ground running" with the charity. Describing the organization's work and her role within it, Meghan said, "Even if it's doing it quietly behind the scenes, which is what I've focused my energy on thus far, meeting with the right people, meeting with the organizations behind the scenes quietly, learning as much as I can, so I can maximize the opportunity we have here to really make an impact."

THE HUBB COMMUNITY
KITCHEN COOKBOOK

Meghan's first solo philanthropic project as a
Royal, launched to the public in September 2018,
was a particularly heartfelt choice. A book of
recipes developed directly with women affected by
the catastrophic Grenfell Tower fire in June 2017,
which killed 72 people and robbed many more of
their homes.

The Hubb Community Kitchen, named for the
word "love" in Arabic, was founded in West London
shortly after the disaster, when displaced women
sought a place to cook fresh, warm food for their
families. Since then, this kitchen has become a
home-from-home which, in the words of the
Duchess, provides the women with a place, "to laugh,
grieve, cry and cook together" as well
as tasting "the memory of home, albeit homes some
had recently lost."

The idea for a Hubb cookbook, containing many of
the kitchen's favourite recipes, came from Meghan
herself after she began secretly volunteering there
and got to know many of the women behind the
initiative. Upon discovering that funding limitations
meant the kitchen could only open two days a week,
the Duchess decided a book would be a great way to
help raise money so that the kitchen could open daily.

In a speech at the launch of the cookbook, Meghan
evocatively described the experience of working in the
space: "The kitchen buzzes with women of all ages;
women who have lived and seen life; laughing, chatting,
sharing a cup of tea and a story, while children play
on the floor or are rocked to sleep in their strollers."
And inside *Together: Our Community Cookbook*, the
Duchess also writes about her own vivid childhood food
memories, praising "the power of a meal to take you to
places you've never been, or transport you right back to
where you came from."

SURVIVORS' NETWORK AND JOFF YOUTH CENTRE

On 4 October 2018, adoring crowds met the Duke and Duchess of Sussex on their first official visit to the county that features in their royal titles. While in Sussex, the couple took time to focus on charities helping rape survivors and those with mental health issues – continuing their previous work in both these areas. Meghan and husband Harry first visited the Survivors' Network in Brighton, a charity in the city that supports survivors of rape and sexual assault, helping around 1,500 people each year. Explaining the "mood of real jubilation in the office" to *BBC. co.uk*, Jay Breslaw, the charity's director, said, "We recognize the huge importance to us [of this visit] as a small charity in Sussex, and particularly in this time when funding is difficult, funds are being cut."

The couple later stopped off at the coastal town of Peacehaven to visit the Joff Youth Centre and hear about its work on mental health and well-being. The Duke and Duchess spent time here with some of the young people who use the centre, which functions both as a relaxation and activity space – and joined in discussions and games that revolved around mental health issues.

Lee Keeley, 16, a visitor to the youth centre, said to *theargus.co.uk*: "They responded so well to all our personal comments about being kept in care. Meghan gave such amazing responses when I opened up about my own experiences and the hard things I have been through. It was really powerful talking to them." Centre manager Libby King, 35, commented on the emotional nature of the royal couple's visit, and the empathetic way in which they interacted with the young people at the centre. "They were so down-to-earth," she told *theargus. co.uk*. "The day was incredibly emotional, especially the moment Meghan and Harry were sat in a circle listening to the young ones opening up about their hard times. At that point I started to well up. They were just so non-judgmental and really listened. They are such an inspiring couple."

THE ROYAL TOUR OF AUSTRALIA AND NEW ZEALAND, FIJI AND TONGA

October 2018 saw Meghan and Harry embark on their first official overseas trip, a 16-day tour during which they attended over 70 different engagements in four different countries. This travel marathon was made more impressive by the announcement, right at the start, that Meghan was pregnant with their first child.

Just as Princess Diana's first tour to Australia with Prince Charles proved a seminal trip, 25 years later Meghan's news ensured the eyes of the world were upon her. It was therefore fitting that the couple chose to spend significant time with key local mental health charities as well as attend the Invictus Games – the sporting event created by Prince Harry in which Armed Forces personnel, previously wounded in combat, compete for their country. Here are two of the causes the couple decided to bring attention to on the tour.

LEFT: At Pillars, a charity operating across New Zealand that supports children who have a parent in prison.

OPPOSITE TOP: Speaking on a visit to the University of the South Pacific, Suva, Fiji.

OPPOSITE BELOW: Greeting locals in a traditional 'hongi' at the formal powhiri and luncheon held at Te Papaiouru Marae, Rotorua, New Zealand.

ONEWAVE, SYDNEY

On 19 October, Meghan and Harry visited OneWave, a local surfing community on Bondi Beach dedicated to raising awareness for mental health and well-being in an engaging way. The couple sat in the sand with the informal surf group that gathers weekly to discuss their personal struggles in what was one of the most intimate moments of the trip.

Harry has previously been very open about dealing with the loss of his mother, Princess Diana, and during this beach session he apparently revealed the important role Meghan has played in helping him process his feelings. "Harry talked about the fact that he spent a long time to try to find someone to talk to, to have those conversations around mental health and it was really beautiful because they found each other," said surfer and group member Charlotte Connell, to CBS News.

MARANUI CAFE, NEW ZEALAND

On 29 October, as the royal tour drew to a close, Meghan and Harry had tea at the Maranui Cafe in Wellington with young people from a number of mental health projects operating in New Zealand, which offer support to other young people through helplines, social media, websites and school-based programmes. While there, Meghan spoke about a topic she has written about before – the sometimes damaging relationship between your sense of self-esteem and social media. "You see photos on social media and you don't know whether she's born with it or maybe it's a filter," explained the Duchess, "Your judgment of your sense of self-worth becomes really skewed when it's all based on likes." The couple also talked to schoolchildren outside the café – with Meghan later running back inside to ask that the leftover cakes be taken out for the children. Some onlookers felt that this simple, thoughtful gesture was an indication that pregnancy was already encouraging her maternal instincts to blossom.

PERSONAL PASSION: MEGHAN'S RECIPE FOR A NEW KIND OF ROYAL

As the newly minted Duke and Duchess of Sussex, Meghan and Prince Harry have now joined the Duke and Duchess of Cambridge as the current and the future public face of the Royal Family. With the Queen now in her nineties and reducing the number of high profile appearances she makes, this younger generation of royals is the new guard – and they are tackling their global roles in a strikingly modern activist style.

The best example of their highly engaged approach is the quartet's joint venture, The Royal Foundation. The causes the foursome are focusing on – including working with young people with mental health issues and protecting the environment – have a more personal emphasis, a notable departure from the work of either the Queen or Prince Charles. A better comparison perhaps is Harry's mother, Princess Diana, who pioneered the informal, very human touch that the young royals display today.

Meghan's experience as both a precocious feminist and a biracial woman and have shaped her beliefs for many years, and if becoming a Duchess is bound to change her in some ways, it's also clear that her unique perspective will also play a large role in the ongoing evolution of the royal family itself.

As the Duchess leaves behind acting to focus on philanthropic work, it seems likely Meghan will continue to enjoy all the interests she displayed during the five years in which she wrote her lifestyle blog *The Tig*. After all, as we have explored in the preceding chapters, her deep love of fashion, beauty, cooking and dining, yoga and travel are all a fundamental part of "being Meghan".

One clear sign that the Duchess of Sussex will continue to combine her personal enthusiasms with charitable royal interests was the September 2018 launch of the book of recipes developed with women affected by the catastrophic London Grenfell Tower fire. Similarly, her visits in October 2018 with Prince Harry to charities dedicated to helping young people with mental health issues, in both Sussex in the UK

and in New Zealand, suggest this area of work, known to be very close to Harry's heart, is one that the couple will continue to focus on together.

The very personal nature of these newer charitable ventures indicates the levels of warmth and direct involvement we can expect Meghan to continue to bring to her public role as a royal. And now, with the birth of their first baby imminent, that future includes becoming a parent with her husband, Prince Harry.

It's abundantly clear to observers that Meghan will want to be as hands-on a mother as she is an activist. Following the example of her sister-in-law, the Duchess of Cambridge, Meghan will doubtless combine the role of new mum effortlessly with her public duties – approaching both with equal joy and enthusiasm. Will Meghan challenge royal convention in ways that even Kate did not? Only time will tell. But as the first biracial woman to marry into the royal family, as well as the first to have had a successful career and the first self-proclaimed feminist, we can be sure that the unique experience of this free spirit from California will leave a profound mark on the future of the monarchy.

Indeed, one of the reasons our new royal is so compelling to watch is because she is so different from princesses past. Around the world, British royalty will continue to represent impossible glamour, pomp and ceremony, but these days we also want our royal role models to be real and relatable, informal and accessible – and in Meghan we have a Duchess who combines the very best traditions with this exciting new future.

INDEX